Defy Average

A High Schooler's Guide to Unlocking Your Best Self

Scott Zellmann

Remember, average is crowded.
You were not meant to be average!

To request permission, please email:
defyaveragebook@gmail.com
Website: defyaveragebook.com

ISBN (paperback): 979-8-218-83028-1
ISBN (hardcover): 979-8-218-83030-4
ISBN(e): 979-8-218-83029-8
Printed in the USA

Edited by: Samantha Salzinski

Cover Design: Scott Zellmann, Inspired Publishing L.L.C.

Contents

Introduction

Before You Begin

Why Journal? The Problem of a Leaky Brain

I've always loved reading, but I realized that a month after finishing a book, the best ideas would slip away. My brain was like a leaky bucket. Journaling is how you patch the holes. It helps you capture insights, organize your thoughts, and reflect on your growth, both now and in the future.

What You'll Need

1. **A Dedicated Journal:** It can be a leather-bound book, a basic notebook, or a digital document. The

key is to have one secure place for all your thoughts.

2. **A Capture Tool:** Always have a notecard, sticky note, or even the notes app on your phone handy while reading. This is for quick thoughts you'll transfer to your journal later.

The 3-Step Method

1. **Mark the Margin:** As you read, if a sentence or idea resonates with you, put a small dot in the margin next to it.

2. **Jot Down the Page:** On your notecard (which can double as your bookmark), write down the page number of each dot you make.

3. **Journal in Short Bursts:** When you have 15-20 minutes, open your journal. Write the date and the book title. Then, go to the page numbers

on your notecard and write down the quotes or your thoughts on them. This isn't a chore; it's a flexible process. Do it when it feels right.

As you start your personal journey with this book, dive in completely. Don't hesitate to make notes, underline your favorite parts, and make it personal. Enjoy the journey and the insights that await you. Remember, this isn't just a task—it's an adventure in self-discovery, growth, and defying average!

Scott Zellmann

Preface

The Story You Don't See

Everyone you meet has a story to tell or one they are living right now. Understanding these stories is essential, as it promotes empathy and connection — two powerful tools that can transform relationships and promote personal growth. This understanding of both empathy and personal connection can make you more aware and conscious of your daily decisions, leading to a more intentional and fulfilling life. Nobody goes through life without experiencing both fantastic moments and moments of heartbreak.

Do not judge my decisions until you know my choices.

— Unknown

This is one of the many reasons I decided to write this book, a collection of my 60 years of life experience and 35 years of working and coaching young people. I have had and shared moments on both sides of the emotional aisle. I have shared moments with students that bring the utmost joy, as well as the saddest moments of despair. Always keep in mind that before we are quick to judge a person, they have a story that we are not aware of, so be sensitive toward them.

Conduct yourself with grace, compassion, support, and care. You will make a difference in their day. Listen first before deciding on your next word, comment, or action, as it matters to those you encounter every day. Remember, everybody has a story, and you don't know it.

Small Choices Over Time

If you drink a can of soda today, nothing changes. Your health is the same, and the choice feels insignificant. But repeat that tiny choice every day for 10 years, and the compounding effect will transform your health for the worse. This principle, however, also works in your favor. Small, consistent choices always add up.

Your daily choices are deposits into the bank of who you will become tomorrow.

Think of your habits like compound interest in a bank account. Investing a single dollar today won't make you rich. However, if you deposit a dollar every day, it begins to earn interest. Soon, your interest starts earning its own interest. Over time, that tiny, consistent deposit grows into a fortune. Your daily choices are deposits into the bank of who you will become tomorrow. This same rule of small inputs leading to massive outputs applies to your direction in life. Imagine a plane taking off from New York headed for California. If the pilot's course is off by just **one degree**, the aircraft will land more than 69 miles away from its intended destination. That one degree felt like nothing at takeoff, but it determined the final destination.

Your daily habits are your one-degree adjustments. Consider the diverging paths they create:

- Choosing to read for 15 minutes instead of scrolling social media.
- Swapping one sugary drink for a bottle of water.
- Review your class notes for 10 minutes before starting a video game.
- Choosing to say an encouraging word instead of gossiping.

These choices seem small, but they are steering you toward a completely different future. The person who makes those small, positive choices every day will, over time, become unrecognizable to the person who doesn't. The question is straightforward: Are your habits pointed toward the destination you want?

The Mental Jail of Mistakes

Mistakes happen, and they are part of being human. The thing about mistakes is that **you** often feel embarrassed and inadequate when **you** make them. Why do **you** feel this way? Because you're human. You know logically that everyone makes mistakes, but you rarely feel that way emotionally.

With the right mindset, mistakes are opportunities for learning. Don't let past mistakes keep you in a mental prison. Ruminating and feeling bad about them is time served in a prison of your own making. Please stop talking to yourself negatively. You need to learn from your mistakes, ask for forgiveness, and move forward.

You don't get to repeat the same mistake and walk away without consequence. A mistake repeated is a choice. If **you** treat a friend poorly because you're upset about something, **you** can apologize and hopefully be forgiven. That was a mistake, and it's a chance for **you** to learn how to treat people when things are not going well. If **you** continue to treat that friend poorly, it will eventually harm the nature of the friendship.

A mistake repeated is a choice.

The mindset **you need** is that mistakes happen, so **you** must own them, apologize for them, learn from them, and then move on. Mistakes in **your** life will tend to repeat themselves until you learn from them. Pay attention and use them as opportunities for personal growth. This resilient and growth-oriented mindset will help **you** navigate life's challenges and setbacks with confidence and determination.

Shaping Your Life with Your Inner Dialogue

Think back to the last time you faced a tough challenge—like running the mile in gym class or starting a big project. Why is it that some people push through the discomfort, while others, who are just as capable, give up? It all comes down to the most important conversation you'll ever have: the one happening inside your own head.

People who listen to themselves often stop. Their mind hears the body's complaints—"this is too hard," "I'm tired," or "I can't do this"—and it quits. But people who talk to themselves are the ones who finish. They actively feed themselves encouragement: "Just one more step." "You've got this." "Keep going."

This internal dialogue isn't random; it follows a clear pattern that determines your success or failure. If you want to change your results, you have to understand and take control of these five steps:

1. **Programming:** From the day you were born, your mind has been programmed by your experiences, your environment, and what others have told you about yourself. If you were constantly told you were "shy" or "not good at math," then programming becomes the foundation of your self-concept.

2. **Beliefs**: Your programming creates your beliefs. It's important to understand that a belief doesn't have to be true to be powerful—you just have to *believe* it's true. If your programming says you're not a natural leader, you will accept it as fact and won't step up when given the chance.

3. **Attitude:** Your beliefs directly shape your attitude. If you believe you're bad at math, your attitude toward a new algebra assignment will be negative and defeated before you even start. You'll approach it expecting to fail.

4. **Feelings:** Your attitude creates your feelings. A defeated attitude toward math will make you feel anxious, frustrated, or bored whenever you have to do it. These feelings are a direct result of the beliefs you hold.

5. **Action (or Inaction):** Your feelings determine your actions. Because you feel anxious and frustrated, you will

procrastinate on your math homework, avoid asking for help, and tune out in class. This action—or lack of it—is what ultimately creates your poor results, reinforcing the original belief that you're "bad at math."

This cycle can feel impossible to break, but the good news is that you are in control. You have the power to interrupt this pattern by changing what you say to yourself. By intentionally using positive and encouraging language when talking to yourself, you can reprogram your mindset. This new programming will build stronger beliefs, leading to a better attitude, more positive feelings, and ultimately, successful actions that will change the course of your life. (The Shaping Your Life with Your Inner Dialogue section is paraphrased from *What To Say When You Talk To Your Self* by Shad Helmstetter, pages 46-52.)

Your Feelings Aren't the Plan—Discipline Is

Feelings are an essential part of being human. They bring immense value to our lives and can feel like a rollercoaster, which is often what makes a day memorable. Without sadness, you wouldn't value happiness; without sorrow, you wouldn't appreciate joy. Each emotion gives life balance.

However, one thing I firmly believe is that feelings are not a reliable guide for action. Science tells us that people react emotionally first and logically second. So when I hear students say, "I don't feel like  doing it," I tell them, "I believe you." Most of the time, the hardest part is just getting started. If you can push past that initial feeling of not wanting to do something, you'll get going and usually finish strong.

As you grow, you learn to harness your emotions. The goal isn't to ignore how you feel, but to build the willpower and discipline to act anyway. Discipline is not a punishment; it sets you free. It's an internal strength you must build to master your emotions and tackle any challenge, regardless of how you feel in the moment.

Let's look at how discipline can set you free with one of the most essential habits for your quality of life: **sleep**. Good, consistent sleep habits move you closer to the best version of yourself and can lead to a longer lifespan, as sleep affects nearly every aspect of your physical and mental health. Poor sleep habits can reduce focus, cause memory problems, increase the risk of Alzheimer's disease, accelerate brain aging, and lead to mood changes. To get the benefits of sleep, you must be disciplined about it, which means limiting caffeine, avoiding electronics before bed, and going to sleep at a consistent time.

Over time, the benefits of good sleep are immense. They include a reduced risk of chronic disease, a stronger immune system, improved mood and emotional stability, enhanced cognitive function, and increased energy levels. This simple—but not always easy—discipline sets you up to win the day. The same is true for other habits, such as nutrition. The small, disciplined choices you make today will either lift you or drag you down in the long run.

Winning Your Inner Dialogue

I find it sad when people who are kind and friendly to others are unkind to themselves. They share compliments, offer encouragement, and root for everyone, yet still find time to be unkind to themselves. They root for everyone else and speak in such an uplifting way. Still, in their internal dialogue, they are critical, harsh, and lack confidence by frequently comparing themselves to others and feeling less than they are, unaware of their authentic and unique value as a person.

You need to talk to yourself more than you listen to yourself.
— Attributed to D. Martyn Lloyd-Jones

When you do talk to yourself, please control the dialogue, keep it positive, and remind yourself to be kind. An example of one of my internal dialogues that I constantly have is that when things get stressful, I remind myself to focus only on what I can control. This allows me to let things go. I still get caught up worrying about things outside of my control, but I have said this enough to myself that I have made it a habit, and it allows me to move forward and lower my stress level. It will take time to change the dialogue in your head, but you can start by doing small, kind things for others, like offering a compliment or a sincere thank you. These acts create a positive foundation, and when your internal dialogue starts to stray, you can reflect on the good you're doing. Win the day, then win enough days in a row, and you will become kinder to yourself. But before we dive into the specific habits and mindsets, it's essential you know where this advice comes from—a journey that started far from where you might think.

Our expedition will unfold in three parts: first, we'll build your Foundation with powerful habits; next, we'll shape your Mindset for greatness; and finally, we'll provide you with Mindsets in Action to bring it all to life.

Scott Zellmann

Discipline is not a punishment;
it sets you free.

Part 1: The Foundation

In this first section, we'll build the foundation for your journey. Before we can build, we have to understand where we're starting from. You'll read my personal story of struggling to defy average and learn about the non-negotiable "anchor habits" that will become the bedrock of your success.

Chapter 1: My Journey

You must remain focused on your journey to greatness.

— Les Brown

1.67 and 19 are numbers. In the spring of my junior year of high school, I met with my high school counselor. In the past, I had rarely met with him, and we never developed a good student-counselor relationship. He never took the time to get to know me. When I entered his office on this particular visit, he quickly closed the door behind me. I went to sit in a chair, and then he sat at his desk. I had no idea what to expect next as we hardly ever met. We talked very briefly, and then he said, "Scott, you are not college material." I didn't know how to respond, so I listened to find out what was going on. In my mind, I already had a brother and a sister in college; it was implied that we would attend college, as I didn't know what else to do. He then told me he would set up a meeting at the Armed Forces recruiting center for me. I have great respect for the Armed Forces. This feeling has only deepened as I've grown older and learned about the daily sacrifices made by those who keep our country safe. People serving in our Armed Forces will never receive enough appreciation. But in my mind, I wanted to play basketball.

Because I was a follower and didn't have many individual thoughts or direction about my future, I visited the Marine Corps Recruiter's Office. I sat down to talk with a recruiter for a while. He then asked me to take a few written tests, which I did gladly, and then he scored them. Then he turned to me and said I could be anything in the Marines I chose to be. I felt good about myself at that moment, knowing I had options despite how my counselor made me feel. I then recalled the Marine recruiter pulling out six plaques and putting them on the desk. He asked me to put them in order of importance, which I quickly did. I didn't think much about it at the time, but I ranked belonging to the US military at the bottom of my current desires. Sensing my hesitation, he asked why I ranked it so low and pointed out that I might not be a good fit for the Marines if that's how I truly felt.

I asked him if there was a basketball team in the Marines that I could join; that was my laser-like focus. He responded that they have intramurals, which is all they have. I told him how important it was for me to play basketball. I wanted to play on a team or in college, which was my dream. He then looked at me and said he did not feel the Marines were a good fit for me, and I agreed. A lot changed in that moment, but I was unaware of it at the time. That experience taught me the importance of believing in myself and the power of having a clear vision for my future.

When I was young, basketball saved my life. It was the one thing I lived for, and it sustained me throughout my high school years. I lived to play, which was all I thought and dreamed about as a child. I read, watched, and played as much as I could during my childhood. I often reflect on how and why that happened, so I decided to write this book to empower young people who need support, guidance, insight, and encouragement in their school experience. A school journey that will one day end, leading them into life after schooling. But your education doesn't stop after graduation, as the responsibility to continue then falls to each individual. Your education should never end. I realized what I was missing as I reflected on my journey and the lessons I had learned.

I am now a retired middle school teacher, currently working as an executive functioning coach at an excellent high school. Executive functioning skills help students organize, plan, chunk (break down into smaller parts) assignments, stay balanced, prioritize, complete work outside the classroom, and more. Things have come full circle, and I want you to know you will make it, and you can do it. Remember, mentorship is essential in your long-term success. Seek guidance and support, and you will find your way. This book serves as a form of mentorship, providing advice to help you navigate your unique path. Get busy reading, as your future self will thank your current self. Reading for life is the continuation of your education. High achievers read extensively to gain a deeper understanding of the world and to challenge their mindset. You need to join that path.

Regarding the numbers at the start of this book, 1.67 is my cumulative GPA from high school, and 19 is my ACT score. Neither is impressive, but they did not define who I was or what my potential could allow me to become. This should enable you to feel optimistic and open-minded. You can still have the life you want despite rough beginnings in the classroom. Don't let anyone tell you that positive things cannot happen; they can and will. I learned that consistently small changes equal significant results over time. What I lacked from junior high through high school was executive functioning skills. However, with self-discipline and determination, I was able to overcome these challenges and achieve success. Remember, it's essential to pursue your passions. They can lead you to places you never thought possible. My love for basketball not only shaped my high school experience but also opened doors to opportunities I never imagined. Your passions have the power to transform your life, so don't be afraid to chase them.

Your passions have the power to transform your life, so don't be afraid to chase them.

My early school years were great. In my K-6 elementary school, where everything took place in one classroom, I excelled and felt like a leader. But when I entered 7th grade, everything changed. The next six years were a struggle because I lacked the basic executive functioning skills to keep up. I became a follower, drifting through classes and getting by with poor grades because I was disorganized, had no adult support, and didn't know how to ask for help.

I played basketball in 7th and 8th grade on the junior high team. I know other students liked to play, but I loved to play. My issue was being six feet tall and about 108 pounds. The more mature boys on the team often pushed me around during practice and games. I was the 7th or 8th player on the junior high team. I was always quite nervous when I played due to my lack of confidence, and as a result, I never performed very well. But that did not deter me as I practiced and played anywhere and anytime I could. I just loved to play.

My first year of basketball mirrored my 8th-grade experience. I had good skills, but I was often pushed around by more physically mature boys on the team and felt the same stress while playing. Although I didn't stand out as a player, I loved playing anytime, anywhere. Today, I reflect on these experiences to help and support students in similar situations.

My sophomore year of high school was different. I had a basketball coach who was very direct and demanding, and I loved it. He knew how to teach and coach basketball. He was not shy about calling anyone out, and he challenged me by telling me I couldn't do something on the court in a testing manner. Practice was always a challenge, and I am very motivated by people doubting me. That always triggers me, and still does, to play as hard as I possibly can. The difference is he believed in me; I could feel it. I started occasionally on the sophomore A team and gained a few pounds, now standing at 6'2". I recall weighing an athletic 130 pounds. I finally got consistent playing time and did pretty well. My family had known my sophomore coach for years, and they trusted him. I finally felt someone pushing me out of their belief in me. It had been a long time to wait for that, and it would be a long time before it happened again.

I had a nice sophomore season overall. I sometimes started, and my skill set advanced, allowing me to increase my playing time. All my year-round playing was finally paying off on the court, but not in the classroom. I passed all my classes except one. I failed geometry in semester 1. That was the one class I failed in high school. Geometry might as well have been a foreign language; it simply never clicked.

My confidence also grew because I got to play in the sophomore B games. I would always show up just to watch, and the B-team coach would ask me to play since he only had seven players on the team. I loved it. I would have done anything to play in those B games because I finally got to play with no strings attached. I was free out there, and I felt so alive. I would start and play almost the whole game. All my friends were on the B team, so it clicked when we worked together as teammates. I remember feeling freer than I ever had on the court; I could just relax and play. I often scored 18-20 points per game. My confidence grew, and I was having fun on the court like never before. It didn't last long, as my joy of playing unrestrained came to an end when the season concluded.

My junior year of high school was a repeat of my sophomore year in the classroom, as it was a continued struggle. I felt intelligent, but I still lacked executive functioning skills and self-discipline. I never really felt good about myself, despite being popular, and I only had the same small group of friends. I thought popularity mattered, but you realize later in life that it doesn't matter at all. Popularity is a perception, and it's often a false one. I wish more students understood that doing things that are not beneficial costs you time and the development of the best version of you. Just do and be you.

My junior year of basketball was another step backward. I was excited to be on the varsity team and thought I could make a valuable contribution. I knew after two days of tryouts that I would make the team. However, I never got the chance to play. Some seniors were good, but I thought I would be in the wings to help the team. I was actually on the bench. I was again back to coaches who did not understand how to connect with each player on a team and develop them throughout the season. As the season started, I did not play, but I did get some action at the JV level. Once again, I did not have any adults to make time to connect with and mentor me, either in the classroom or on the court. I did pass all my classes, however. I knew for sure I wanted to play college basketball. I didn't care where it was, as long as it was at a college.

Senior year arrived, and I was excited for my chance to play regularly. I still hoped to be a highly valued player on the team. I continued to struggle with organizational skills, but I was on schedule to graduate. As the season approached, I now had to compete with many juniors who I felt were not as good as I was, but the coaches found them more likable. I still think it was political. My coach started me in most games, but I came out as soon as I made a mistake. I quickly adopted the mindset of avoiding errors—an approach that, in fact, is an awful one, since mistakes are an inevitable part of the game. I usually made a mistake early in the game, and I was usually the first one out.

None of that is what caring looks like.

The final straw for me losing respect for my coach was when we were winning by 10-12 points against a team. I stole the ball on a cross-court pass as the weak-side wing in our 1-3-1. I dribbled without a defender in front of me. I took off, tried to dunk the ball too hard, and missed. The coach pulled me out of the game and sat me out for the rest of the game. After the game, his only words were, "You will run a mile after every practice until I say you are done." I only had to run one mile, and then he forgot. It made little sense why I had to run, but his forgetting about it stuck with me. It drove it home that he did not care. None of that is what caring looks like. I tell young teachers today that the students who are the hardest to like need the most care, grace, and mercy. The season ended, and I was looking for a place to play basketball.

Having recently started attending a local church more regularly with a friend of mine during my senior year, I ended up attending a church basketball tournament about 45 minutes away at a college. My mindset was that I was going to dominate in that tournament, and I did play very well. I boosted my self-esteem by excelling in the area where I knew I was best. I had a fire inside of me. After a few games, a player at the college who was officiating the games approached me about playing there. In my head, I signed up right there to play collegiate basketball. Coaches from the college started calling me and keeping in touch. I loved it and felt important. I played in the team's basketball summer league, where I learned and grew my confidence. I was again free to play openly and found I had a knack for scoring. I also had a lot to learn playing against bigger and stronger athletes. I finally topped 150 pounds over the summer. I was accepted into Trinity College and arrived for my first year, only to discover that the coaches who had recruited me were no longer there. They had a new coach for the team. I didn't care, as I knew

I could make an impact, and we had a few good players; however, we weren't a deep team with many talented players. When the season started, I was ready. I had gained 25 pounds as a late bloomer and had reached 175 pounds. I was thrilled, and all my practice was paying off.

My new coach, Bruce Fields, became a life mentor and was the first person in my life to sit down and talk to me, despite the challenges of my attitude and arrogance stemming from my success on the court, which I struggled to handle. He changed my life. That is what I want to be for young people. You are being supported to become the best version of you.

Why do I say it was a challenge? I had to take responsibility for who I was at that time. I was not the easiest person to coach or teach. As I retired after 33 and a half years of teaching, it's precisely those challenging young people who need to be shown grace and patience and listened to while being mentored. Those who are the most demanding often require the most patience and encouragement. I never had that, and Bruce provided me with the accountability and balance that I needed. I was yelled at or ignored in junior high and high school. I loved Bruce, and he spoke at my wedding. He was heaven-sent for me and had the right temperament to help me through my struggles. Young people need guidance and support. The world is a complicated place.

Those who are the most demanding often require the most patience and encouragement.

I am writing this book to share with students and parents how they can shape their mindset, habits, and insights in education, as well as the character they should develop. I struggled early on, but I was fortunate to have people who guided and invested in me. We can all be on the lookout to help another person in their life walk. It's a great joy and privilege to walk with young people. They amaze me, and I envy their amazingness. I also met my future wife, Sheron, in my first year at Trinity. She showed me care and support like no one ever had.

A significant detail to note about my first year at Trinity College was that I was placed in a first-semester academic support class to help guide me and maintain my mental balance in each course. It was an executive functioning class before its time. I got off to a good start academically. As my college years progressed, I worked to overcome some significant gaps in my previous learning. I graduated with a Bachelor of Arts degree in Physical Education. I then continued and received a Master of Science degree from the University of Illinois at

Chicago. I secured an excellent job and taught in the same district for 33 and a half years, retiring after a long career. Although I may have retired, I moved on to another job that pushed me to write this book. I am an executive functioning coach at a wonderful high school. I have walked in every step that my students tell me about. It's like looking in a time machine's mirror. I love to help them because it's a path I've traveled and did not enjoy. I want to be there to support students in the early part of their school and life journey. Many young people deeply touch my heart as I strive to help them achieve their best lives.

Your mistakes and stumbles don't define you—they serve you, but only if you learn from them. Looking back, I realized that what I was missing wasn't intelligence or talent—it was a set of simple, powerful routines. I didn't have the foundation I needed. That's why the next chapter is the most important one in this book.

We're going to build that foundation with what I call anchor habits.

If you are persistent, you will get it.
If you are consistent, you will keep it.

— Harvey Mackay

Chapter 2: Anchor Habits

Success is nothing more than a few simple disciplines, practiced every day.

— Jim Rohn

In his book *The Power of Habit*, Charles Duhigg offers a fascinating insight into what he calls "keystone habits." Duhigg defines these as habits that "lead us to make better choices in other parts of our lives." He explains that keystone habits are the building blocks for sound decisions, noting that they "start a process that, over time, transforms everything." A key part of this transformation is the concept of "small wins," which Duhigg says have "enormous power" and "influence disproportionate to the accomplishments of the victory themselves." These small wins "fuel transformative changes by leveraging tiny advantages into patterns that convince people that bigger achievements are within reach." For students trying to improve in school, I use the term "anchor habits" to describe the fundamental routines that support academic success. These are fundamental habits that serve as anchors, helping you become the best version of yourself each day. Consistency always wins; you must build a strong foundation, and nothing sets the tone like an anchor for stability.

Simple and easy are not the same thing.

Anchor habits are not just essential routines; they are the building blocks for the most efficient version of you. There are no shortcuts, and you cannot cheat the process. They take, test, and grow your discipline. It's critical to understand, however, that simple and easy are not the same thing. For example, running six miles is straightforward—you simply run until you've covered the distance. But is it easy? For most people, no.

If you just start, you will be on the path. In a few weeks, the process will take better shape, and you will be in a better place. You need to realize that what works for one person may not work for another. Anchor habits are for everyone, but you must adjust them to fit your specific needs. It's not about following a one-size-fits-all approach, but about finding what works best for you.

Students often use their peers' opinions as an indicator of their future test success, which can create an emotional response, typically worry or anxiety. They may now feel inadequately prepared based on their peers' feedback. This decreases their confidence, and anxiety now takes root in their brain, growing, while their confidence shrinks. Walking in confidently and relaxed is a much better approach to a quiz or a test. Often, students walk in worried because the person they had judged as smart might have said the test was hard. What if the competent person said it was easy, and after taking it, you thought it was hard? Now, how do you feel about yourself? Why do I bring up this scenario? It's because we all look around and mirror the behavior of other students, following what is trending. It does not make it a good thing just because everyone else is doing it too. I was a long-time follower in high school, and I gave away my power just by trying to fit in instead of doing what I needed to do to grow my confidence and success. Instead, I followed. Before we delve into anchor habits, I would like to share some insights on habit development. It's fascinating to know that when you're born, you have no habits. Consider that everything you do routinely has become a habit for one reason or another. Sometimes we do things and wonder why we continuously do them. Most often, it's a habit, good or bad. We enjoy good habits and need to replace bad habits, but that will take some time to do. How about a mindset for adopting a new habit and becoming a better version of yourself that can handle anything that comes your way?

It is fascinating to know that when you are born, you have no habits.

Imagine I asked you to run six miles, and your immediate reaction was "I can't do that" or "I won't do that." This response is likely due to a lack of preparation or a negative experience with running. But what if I asked you to run just a quarter mile? Your response would probably be "I can do that." This shift in mindset toward success is what discipline is all about. Don't let the task at hand determine your mindset; that is for you to choose. You might think that a quarter-mile run won't make a difference, but over time, it will. So, run a quarter of a mile for three days in a row—a small habit success. Start small and keep it small. Be the person who starts small with no excuses. Then, run a half mile three more days in a row. As your confidence and success grow, so does the likelihood that you will stick with the new habit. Then three-quarters of a mile for three more days. In just nine days, you've started making gains and tipping your mindset toward success. This is the power of discipline, of setting and achieving small goals, of taking control of your life and your success. No one who has accomplished great things has ever gotten anywhere by being embarrassed by starting small. The success of your narrative relies on the building blocks. You have the power to shape your academic success.

That ability to start small and stay committed is the foundation of discipline. Anchor habits are the foundation for building discipline into your daily life, ensuring you move forward even when you don't feel like it.

What will stop you? Comparison can and often does. Comparison discourages people from feeling good about themselves and their progress, as it causes them to feel "less than" and defeated. As Teddy Roosevelt said, "Comparison is the thief of joy." Think about the constant comparison engine of social media, ads, and the classroom; it consistently makes you feel envious and discouraged. The time it takes you to meet your 6-mile running goal is your time and only your time. It's nobody else's business. When we talk to ourselves, we control the conversation—when we listen to ourselves, the conversation controls us. Think about that again. Continuously talking to ourselves with positive comments is what we need to do all the time. We then need to listen to ourselves less over time. Remember, your life is unique, and your progress is what matters. Stay focused on your journey and your progress, and don't let comparison steal your confidence and happiness in your pursuit of academic development.

You need to talk to yourself more than you listen to yourself.

What Your Best Version Looks Like

The concept of the "best version of you" refers to an ideal self that encompasses one's fullest potential—physically, mentally, emotionally, and spiritually. This definition highlights various aspects that contribute to personal growth and fulfillment.

First, the best version of you involves self-awareness. This means understanding your strengths, weaknesses, values, and motivations. It encompasses a commitment to continuous learning and self-improvement, allowing you to adapt and grow through life experiences.

Emotionally, the best version of yourself includes growing resilience and emotional intelligence. This means being able to manage your emotions, understand others' feelings, and form healthy relationships. It encourages empathy, compassion, and the ability to communicate effectively.

In terms of health, the best version of you prioritizes physical well-being. This can encompass maintaining an active lifestyle, eating a balanced diet, and ensuring mental health through practices such as mindfulness and stress management.

Spiritually, this idea embraces personal beliefs and a sense of purpose. It challenges individuals to explore their values and passions, paving the way for greater fulfillment. Whether through personal reflection, spirituality, or a connection with nature, this aspect can also contribute to an enriched life experience.

Lastly, the best version of you is often about fostering relationships and contributing positively to society. It involves inspiring others, engaging with your community, and leaving a positive impact on the world around you.

In summary, the best version of you is a holistic blend of self-awareness, emotional maturity, physical health, spiritual fulfillment, and social responsibility—each element working in harmony to create a more balanced and fulfilling life.

Anchor Habits You Need

Sleep

You need to sleep 8-10 hours a night. The usual reaction is that I don't have time to sleep because I'm so busy. I'm sure you're busy, but you need to prioritize your anchor habits, and sleep has to be at the top of the list. When you find yourself drifting away in class, struggling to concentrate, experiencing poor recall, and feeling tired, a lack of sleep is usually the culprit. Did you know that you process the events of the day into long-term memory when you sleep? Lack of sleep is associated with reduced memory and increased brain fog. Pumping up the caffeine is not a good solution for making up for lost sleep. It may work in the short term, but it's not a sustainable solution. How can you be the best you can be without being mentally sharp?

Think of your brain like a busy city. During the day, it's bustling with activity, which creates a lot of "mental trash"—waste products from all that thinking. The glymphatic system is your brain's nighttime cleaning crew. When you sleep, this crew comes out and

power-washes the streets of your brain, clearing out all that junk so you can start fresh the next day. If you don't get enough sleep, the trash piles up. That's what brain fog is—you're trying to navigate a city full of yesterday's garbage.

To summarize, the glymphatic system is a mechanism that removes waste from the brain during sleep. Interestingly, people often overlook the importance of quality sleep when experiencing fatigue, lack of concentration, reduced drive, and creativity, among other symptoms. Quality sleep sets the table for many things. To feel better every day, focus on your sleep process each night.

Here are some helpful ideas:

- No eating 2 hours before bed
- No fluids 1 hour before bed
- Turn your phone off 1 hour before bed
- Block the blue light on your devices 2 hours before bed (if you don't know what that is, search it)
- Try to go to bed at a consistent time each night (consistency wins)
- Before you go to sleep, write a list of things you need to do tomorrow to clear your brain to be able to relax and sleep
- Try to sleep in a cool room
- Block ambient light

- DO NOT have your phone in your room. The temptation to check it leads to more screen time, which hinders your ability to establish a good sleep pattern.

 ## Proper Nutrition

I understand that sometimes eating a balanced diet can be challenging. The idea is to plan with your food to help you win the day. When you prepare your food plan ahead of time, you're taking control of what you can to help you both feel and do your best to meet the increasing demands of your schedule.

When you wake up, start your morning with a glass of water. It's **not** a good idea to start your day with a caffeine drink in one hand and your phone in the other. Start your mind and body with what neuroscience currently suggests is the best morning practice that prepares you the most to handle what comes your way. Caffeine and your phone can increase your cortisol level to start your day, but you can avoid this if you follow best practices. There are many good choices to start your day after consuming water. Include a protein in the morning as it will help with satiety and reduce hunger.

Always try to limit your intake of sugar, processed oils, and highly processed foods. Again, you may not notice a difference when you constantly consume them, but like any habit, over time, they will add up to costing you in terms of your long-term health. A good protein source, such as Greek yogurt, is a part of a well-rounded breakfast. You have to develop a good breakfast plan.

You will not wake up and become a certified breakfast nutritionist overnight. Proper nutrition is a process of learning from mistakes and consistently making better choices over time. If you can change one thing a week that you add to your diet, that is an improvement to your wellness. Similarly, subtracting one thing from your diet will also improve it. Work on improving your diet from both ends. Think about how many changes there will be in a month, three months, or a year. It all stacks for you or against you. You have a choice to become educated now or have more health issues later. I work with students who come to school, and one question I often ask them is whether they have eaten breakfast. The answer is frequently "no" because they did not have time. I then ask how they will feel in two hours, with nothing in their stomach to give them energy. Can you pay attention when you're hungry? Usually not. It's an interesting thought: when a store has a dedicated health-food aisle, it makes you wonder about the default nature of what's in the other aisles.

Here are some helpful ideas:

- **Win the day by starting it right:** Plan your breakfast and lay out your clothes the night before.

- **Pack a smart lunch:** Put thought and nutritious food into the lunch you make.

- **Avoid the enemies:** Cut out non-fruit sugars, sodas, and processed meats.

- **Do your research:** Look up terms like "seed oils" and "caffeine half-life."

Exercise

Exercise is finding engaging movements you enjoy each day. It may be a sport, a dance class, running, walking, yoga, Pilates, lifting weights, or something else. I hope that you both make time and find a way to move that brings you joy and helps move you to a better place after participating in it. It is easy in middle school and high school to be active due to the numerous P.E. classes, sports, clubs, and other activities that provide opportunities for participation. Along the way, find and seek something that will keep you moving as you age. What are two long-term activities that you can stay engaged in when you are no longer in school? I have taken up walking and hiking, which I do routinely. My competitive nature often prompts me to challenge myself, so I walk 4 to 10 miles at a time, at a pace of about 15 to 16 minutes per mile.

As I type this, I want to share that when I started, I was averaging around 20 minutes per mile and only doing 2 to 3 miles at a time. The lesson to learn from this is to get started and see where it takes you and how you progress. That process is exciting and rewarding. I also personally enjoy rucking (the action of walking with weight on your back) and working my upper body with a macebell, clubbell, and kettlebell. I have also added hitting a heavy bag to mix it up. I chose these activities because I had no prior experience with them; they challenged me, which caused me to struggle and grow. I enjoy the challenge of improving because I see the benefits down the road, and I stay disciplined and excited to pursue further improvement. Think about finding a new exercise hobby that will challenge you, and you can find personal growth in it.

The hardest part of exercise sometimes is just getting started.

The second part of examining exercise is the need for supporting balance in life and your overall wellness. Exercise requires self-discipline and is a valuable asset for everyone to learn. The hardest part of exercise is getting started. Pick something you find helpful that you can do conveniently. My exercise scheme works for my schedule because it can all be done at my convenience and around my house. It also has zero ongoing monthly costs.

Exercise has profound mental and emotional benefits, including:

- Reduced anxiety and depression
- Stress relief
- Increased self-esteem
- Improved sleep quality
- Social connections
- Reduction in stress hormones
- Brain chemistry
- Improved cognitive function

We often know the physical benefits of exercise, but that list shows a fantastic way to enhance your life. Just get started, focus on consistency, and enjoy the benefits. If you feel tired, going for a walk will revive you very quickly. Try it a few times and see what happens. View exercise as preventive medicine or as part of a recovery plan. It's all about a mindset. Either way, make it part of your routine. Exercise is one thing you can do to start your day on a winning note! Win enough days, and a better version of you will arrive over time.

Here are some helpful ideas:
- **Find exercises you enjoy.**
- **Aim for 4-5 days a week.**
- **Make time for it**—it has to be a priority.
- **Start small;** any step is better than no step.
- **Keep it fresh** by finding multiple ways to exercise.

Reading

"I don't like to read." "I don't have time." "I already have enough school reading."

These are common reasons for avoiding one of life's most powerful anchor habits. Often, the real reason isn't a lack of time but a self-limiting belief. I once worked with a student who, before even starting an article, told me, "I'm a slow reader." She had repeated this thought in her head so many times that it became her truth—a glass ceiling she had built for herself.

The simplest way to shift from a fixed to a growth mindset is by adding one small word to your self-talk: yet.

— Carol Dweck

This is a perfect example of what Stanford psychologist Dr. Carol Dweck calls a fixed mindset: the belief that your abilities are static and can't be changed. It's the mindset that leads to quitting. The alternative is a growth mindset, which understands that abilities can be developed through dedication and hard work.

The simplest way to shift from a fixed to a growth mindset is by adding one small word to your self-talk: yet. Instead of "I'm a slow reader," the thought becomes, "I'm not as fast a reader as I want to be *yet*."

That single word is the sound of a growth mindset in action. It transforms a dead-end statement into a promise of future progress. It acknowledges the struggle but accepts the challenge. Making reading a consistent habit, even for just 15 minutes a day, is an investment in yourself that compounds over time. The benefits are undeniable: improved focus, increased vocabulary, enhanced writing skills, reduced stress, and ultimately, greater knowledge.

Reading is not a pass/fail test; it is a lifetime practice. It's a fundamental part of your walk to becoming the best version of yourself. Your future self will thank you for taking the first step today.

Here are some helpful ideas:
- Take the time to find something you will enjoy reading.

- Only read 15 pages at a time to stay motivated, 4-5 days a week.
- This allows you to call yourself a reader, and that is a growth mindset.
- Being a reader is not a pass-fail question. The idea is to be a reader.
- If you read 15 pages a day for 5 days a week, that's 3,900 pages a year.
- That is about 15 books a year.
- Consider reading three to four books simultaneously to keep your mind engaged.

Books to read on mindset and inspiration:

- *Chop Wood Carry Water* by Joshua Medcalf
- *Pound the Stone* by Joshua Medcalf
- *The Compound Effect* by Darren Hardy

- *Why the Best Are the Best* by Kevin Eastman
- *Relentless Optimism* by Darrin Donnelly
- *Win the Day* by Mark Batterson
- *Trust the Grind* by Jeremy Bhandari
- *Training Camp* by Jon Gordon
- *High Ten* by Martin Rooney
- *The Twin Thieves* by Steve Jones and Lucas Jadin
- *The Carpenter* by Jon Gordon
- *The Positive Dog* by Jon Gordon
- *The Little Book of Talent* by Daniel Coyle
- *Beyond Basketball* by Mike Krzyzewski with Jamie K. Spatola
- *Think Like a Warrior* by Darrin Donnelly
- *Old School Grit* by Darrin Donnelly
- *Victory Favors the Fearless* by Darrin Donnelly

- *The Turnaround* by Darrin Donnelly
- *The Leadership Playbook* by Jamy Bechler
- *Toughness* by Jay Bilas
- *The Energy Bus* by Jon Gordon
- *Grit* by Angela Duckworth
- *Never Finished* by David Goggins
- *Sustain Your Game* by Alan Stein Jr. with Jon Sternfeld
- *Legacy* by James Kerr
- *Ego Is the Enemy* by Ryan Holiday
- *Stillness Is the Key* by Ryan Holiday
- *Discipline Is Destiny* by Ryan Holiday
- *Soul Food* by Frank Sonnenberg
- *What to Say When You Talk to Your Self* by Shad Helmstetter
- *Mindset* by Carol S. Dweck
- *What Drives Winning* by Brett Ledbetter
- *Man's Search for Meaning* by Viktor E. Frankl

The Five-Friend Rule

Who you hang around with will have a tremendous impact on the direction of your life in both the long and short term. People often say you become the average of the five people you spend the most time with. You need to choose wisely, and most often, we don't give it a second thought in high school. It is not uncommon for people to compromise who they are to belong to a group. High school students are often unskilled in many of the situations they face and are still trying to figure out various aspects of peer groups, including who they want to be and what they stand for. Peer groups make them feel connected, yet sometimes these groups drift into a poor dynamic, and this is how good people wind up making poor choices. They compromise in a moment, crumbling under the pressure of their peers. Errors in judgment usually occur when something unplanned surprises you. Now you're conflicted. If you make plans to go to a movie with a group and they come to pick you up in a car, but the group decides to go to a house party instead. You're now in a moment of intense peer pressure that can put you in a compromising situation.

Another example is the same group frequently having sleepovers, which often turns into a fun time. Then, one night when no adults were around, a group member brought out some vodka. Suddenly, peer pressure to drink increased significantly. Think about it; it's late at night, you've had many sleepovers before, and you feel comfortable. Now, suddenly, a bottle of vodka is being passed your way. You have never had alcohol and were not planning to drink any until the legal age. Your parents have warned you many times about good choices. You also know your parents would be disappointed if they knew you were going along with the group. Many thoughts rush through you. Suppose you call your parents and go home. They're going to wonder what happened. You think, "If I skip drinking some, I may never live it down, and if I do drink some, I will be disappointed in myself for compromising." What choice do you make at that moment? They all seem like "no-win."

Let's back up and see when this situation started. We often think the problem begins when the alcohol is revealed and opened. However, this is not always the case. This is why you need to pay attention to what your social group is about. Has anyone been talking about alcohol recently, even in a joking way? Did anyone ever mention wanting to try it, and did someone agree to it? Not all these situations are preventable, and sometimes we think our friends are just kidding, only to find out they were not. Phones can facilitate poor conversations that might not have otherwise occurred or been continued. It's hard, but sometimes you may need to walk alone to stand up for who you are or want to be in the long run, rather than seeking the approval of a group that may come at a cost in the short run.

A little secret: High school may seem like a long time as part of your life, but it will pass quickly overall and seem less and less important as you get older. Take pride in not compromising who you are to try to fit in. If you have made some mistakes, don't feel bad; use them as lessons to learn from and move on. Look at all the adults you know. They have lessons learned from high school, too. Many adults either don't share their mistakes or have forgotten them. Some adults will share their learning experiences. Consider the fact that a repeated mistake is a choice. Learning is key, and taking responsibility for your actions is essential.

The best way to protect yourself and develop yourself is to be active and involved in high school. This is why schools offer a wide range of extracurriculars. It helps students grow, explore, and use their time and energy wisely. It also promotes accountability, for example, through participation in an athletic team and adhering to the code of conduct. That fosters positive expectations, which in turn lead to positive accountability. Studies show that the more involved you are, the fewer at-risk behaviors high school students can be exposed to.

You will naturally adopt the habits and attitudes of the group you spend the most time with. This happens because our powerful need to belong drives us to mimic the behaviors we observe in order to fit in. This tendency is especially strong in high school, making your choice of friends a critical factor in your personal development. Therefore, choose wisely who you give your time to, as they will directly shape the person you become.

Here are some helpful ideas:

- Get involved early and often.
- Try one club and one sport per year.
- Keep the perspective that you are going after the experience of being involved.
- A club or a sport is a great way to make new social connections that you will have in common.
- It is better to stand for something alone than to fall for everything just to be a member of a group that is not taking you in a good direction.

To close this chapter, remember that some choices will affect you and directly move you in the wrong direction. If you're truly serious about being the best version of yourself, you need to establish daily anchor habits that support that vision. I'm talking about tobacco use, alcohol, vaping, and excessive gaming. These are choices that can subtly move you away from your best version of yourself over time, so that you may not even notice the change occurring. However, remember that you have the power to make these choices. You are not a victim of circumstance. You can choose to be in control of your life and your future. It's worth asking where the idea that alcohol equals a "good time" comes from. Primarily, it stems from society and a multi-billion-dollar industry that has promoted that message for decades. However, the need to be secretive and lie to people you care about creates a gap between the person you are and the person you want to become. That path is in direct opposition to being the best version of yourself, as it's based on deception rather than authenticity. I have directly seen and lived with the horrible effects of alcohol on people and how it affects everyone around them.

Let's be real: the pressure to drink in high school is intense. It feels like it's everywhere—parties, social media, even casual hangouts. It's marketed as the key to having a good time, and the fear of being the only one not doing it is powerful. I get it. But being the best version of yourself means seeing through that illusion. You're being influenced by a multi-billion-dollar industry that doesn't care about your health.

Here's the hard truth they don't show in the ads: Alcohol is a Group 1 carcinogen, just like tobacco. They don't show the car accidents, the assaults, or the sickness. The idea that you need alcohol to have fun is a lie marketed by geniuses. When young people start drinking, it's not a logical choice; it's an emotional one. It becomes a habit that seems harmless at first—like leaving a bicycle out in a light mist overnight; one time does nothing. But make it a habit, and rust slowly and silently takes over, weakening the chain and freezing the gears, until one day the thing you relied on for freedom and movement simply won't work anymore. If you start in high school, chances are you will continue that habit into college.

It is always better to walk alone for a while than to compromise who you are.

You get to choose when you start, but you don't always get to decide how it ends, mainly because the friends you choose can lead you down a path you never would have walked on your own. I tried alcohol for a short while and had my last drink at 23. To this day, I wish I had never tried it. A mistake made once is a lesson, but a repeated mistake is a deliberate choice. Friends who respect your decision to protect your future are the ones worth keeping. You have a choice—make it a wise one with no regrets.

I feel like the evidence for tobacco is so strong about how it affects you in the short and long term that it's a simple, poor choice toward being the best version of you. Evidence of vaping's adverse health effects continues to grow. Over time, I believe studies will confirm its costly impact. It's easy to see the data on all tobacco use and how it will quickly and harshly take you off your best path.

Lastly, there is gaming and the potential it has to absorb us into an altered pixel world that we enjoy, but it risks taking us nowhere when people play for hours upon hours, day after day. Let me clarify that gaming can be both fun and exciting. It can be a great social experience, connecting people and serving as a stress release. What I am critical of is people missing out on life and failing to move forward because of gaming. Sitting on the couch and just playing, not being present, etc.

Another example is going home after school, gaming until the last few minutes of your day, and then cramming in your homework at the worst possible time, when you're tired and short on patience. You don't take the time to learn from your homework; you just do it quickly to get it done. However, you didn't do it in a way that will support tomorrow's learning in class, and so you will slowly start to fall behind. These are my concerns about gaming being a disruptor to your best self. You skip family and friend time, and you also don't read or get much exercise. This type of gaming habit may not seem to have an immediate impact at first. But it's like saving one blurry, useless photo on your phone—it takes up almost no space. Do it every day, however, and you never delete the junk. Eventually, you're left with a device clogged with thousands of meaningless images, and when you try to capture a truly important moment, you can't. You get the "Storage Full" error, having traded precious capacity for worthless clutter. I hope you care enough about yourself to stand tall and be courageous in your life. This is the main reason I wrote this book: to challenge you, allow you to reflect, and think ahead to become great, find the greatness within you, and grow it strong each day. Remember, you're worth the effort. Taking care of yourself is not a selfish act; it is a necessary one. By making healthy choices, you're showing yourself the love and respect you deserve. With these physical and social anchors now in place, we can begin to focus on the character you're trying to build.

We are what we repeatedly do. Excellence, then, is not an act, but a habit.

— Aristotle

Part 2: The Mindset

Section A: The Foundations of Character

With a solid foundation in place, we now turn inward. This section is all about shaping the most powerful tool you have: your mindset. We'll explore what true greatness looks like in school, ask the deeper questions that define you, and learn from the mindsets of some of the most resilient people on the planet.

Chapter 3: What Is Greatness?

Our greatness has always come from people who expect nothing and take nothing for granted—folks who work hard for what they have, then reach back and help others after them.

— Michelle Obama

Greatness isn't some magical quality you're born with. It's what happens when you use your agency, day after day, to choose honor, practice kindness, and show courage. Greatness is achievable in school, as students grow and continue to seek a better version of themselves. I have taught some awe-inspiring young people who caught my eye as a teacher because they possessed greatness at such a young age. How do they catch on to this so early in life? It truly matters, and they have an impact wherever they go just because of who they are. They don't try to be great, but it comes out of their mouth, head, and heart. I think this is possible for everyone. Make it part of your trek and start today. In a month, you will be a different person and will positively impact those around you, helping them to become a better version of themselves. Let's explore the qualities of greatness that are attainable by everyone. It will be a constant pursuit daily with small acts in each area.

Chapter 4: The Power of Honor

No person was ever honored for what he received. Honor has been the reward for what he gave.

— Calvin Coolidge

Honor

 Honor is often described as a set of principles that guide individuals to behave ethically, live with integrity, and uphold their commitments. It embodies values like respect, honesty, fairness, and responsibility. For teenagers at the edge of adulthood, developing a sense of honor is key not only for their personal growth but also for building healthy relationships and fostering a positive community.

During the teenage years, individuals face numerous challenges and peer pressures that can test their character and resilience. Cultivating a sense of honor provides a solid foundation for making wise decisions, standing up for what is right, and navigating the complexities of social interactions. Honor fosters a sense of self-respect and dignity, which can have a profound positive impact on a teenager's mental and emotional well-being. Make sure your words have meaning. Try to make what you say kind, supportive, helpful, and welcoming. Even if you disagree, you can do it with honor. Some examples of honor among students include returning a lost wallet, giving credit for a great play in sports, and stopping rumors when you know the source.

Honor in High School

1. Self-Reflection

The path to developing honor begins with self-reflection. Teenagers should take time to consider their values and what honor means to them. Asking questions like "What do I stand for?" and "How do I want to be perceived by others?" can help clarify personal beliefs and principles. The first step is to build and demand honor within yourself and know where to draw the line for your expectations.

2. Setting Personal Standards

Once teens have a better understanding of their values, they should work to establish personal standards that align with those beliefs. You will make mistakes while working on the process. The mistakes should serve as lessons, not an emotional jail for being imperfect. Learn from mistakes; this is the essence of the growth process. These standards can involve commitments to honesty in communication, fairness in dealing with others, and taking accountability for your actions.

3. Lead by Example

Teenagers can develop their sense of honor by emulating individuals they admire and respect. These could be role models such as family members, teachers, or public figures known for their integrity. Observing and understanding the behaviors that contribute to a person's honorable reputation can provide valuable lessons. The backbone of this is daily character, demonstrating and cultivating your honor over time by practicing it and deepening its roots within you.

4. Engage in Community Service

Participating in community service is another powerful way to cultivate honor. Helping others fosters empathy and reinforces a sense of responsibility. Engaging in activities that contribute to the betterment of the community allows teens to practice honor in action. The act of becoming an integral part of your community enables you to strengthen your community and uplift others along the way, making it a better place to live. Serving others is a blessing and a humbling experience that has a profoundly beneficial impact on your life.

5. Surround Yourself with Positive Influences

The people surrounding a teenager can significantly impact their perception of honor. By choosing friends and mentors who show honorable traits, teens can establish a support system that encourages them to maintain their high standards. I often see young people compromising themselves because of the need to belong. It's said that you become like the five people you spend the most time with. Choose your friends wisely and let them know what you stand for so you can stand together.

6. Embrace Accountability

Learning to take responsibility for one's actions is a vital aspect of developing honor. Teenagers should understand that mistakes are a part of life and that owning up to those errors is a sign of strength, not weakness. This approach builds character and earns respect from peers and adults alike. The sooner you own it, the smaller the issue stays. We often see people blaming others when they are responsible, which damages their character and integrity. If you plan to be a leader long term, you're responsible at the highest level. Learn about it and begin to develop it at a young age to prepare you for the great path you're on.

7. The Wrap-Up

In conclusion, honor is a meaningful quality that young people can develop during their teenage years. By engaging in self-reflection, setting personal standards, leading by example, participating in community service, surrounding themselves with positive influences, and embracing accountability, teenagers can cultivate a strong sense of honor that will guide them throughout their lives. As they navigate the complexities of adolescence, establishing and nurturing this foundational value will serve them well in their travels toward adulthood and beyond.

Chapter 5: The Practice of Kindness

Carry out a random act of kindness, with no expectation of reward, safe in the knowledge that one day someone might do the same for you.

— Attributed to Princess Diana

Kindness

 Kindness can be defined as the quality of being friendly, generous, and considerate. It involves recognizing the struggles of others and taking action to help. In educational settings, such as high school, acts of kindness can significantly enhance the overall atmosphere, fostering a sense of belonging and support among students.

Kindness in High School

1. Mentorship programs: Upperclassmen mentoring first-year students can be a profound example of kindness. By guiding them through challenges and offering advice, they help ease the transition into high school. We often take for granted how much an upperclassman knows about the high school experience, and their sharing is beneficial. As first-year students, we sometimes don't even know what to ask.

2. Support during difficult times: If a classmate is experiencing personal challenges, such as dealing with family issues or loss, showing kindness through modest gestures, like checking in or spending time together, demonstrates empathy and support. When people know that others care and are willing to support them, it is a remarkable moment to face challenges without feeling alone. Sometimes just being there is enough for people to feel encouraged.

3. Random acts of kindness: High school students can surprise others with small acts, such as leaving encouraging notes in lockers, surprising a friend with their favorite snack, or organizing a "Kindness Week" where students perform daily acts of kindness. I would suggest doing kind acts outside of your friend group and making them a regular habit. These also take courage, and when done with great sincerity, are such an uplifting gift to someone's school journey. I would suggest looking for random acts of kindness for people who often go unnoticed but are very kind and helpful.

4. Respecting diversity: Promoting acceptance and understanding across diverse backgrounds and lifestyles is crucial in high school. Students can show kindness by standing up against bullying and supporting campaigns that advocate for inclusivity.

Kindness in high school isn't just a concept—it's essential for creating a positive educational environment. Through various acts and behaviors, students not only enrich their own experiences but also contribute to the well-being of their peers. Encouraging a culture of kindness can lead to lasting friendships and create a community where everyone feels valued and supported.

Chapter 6: Finding Your Courage

You will never do anything in this world without courage. It is the greatest quality of the mind next to honor.

— Aristotle

Courage

Courage in high school can be defined as the ability to confront challenges, make difficult decisions, and act in ways that may be unpopular but are rooted in strong moral values. Courage is not merely the absence of fear, but rather the willingness to act in the face of it.

High school is a unique time when students explore their identities, form friendships, and navigate social dynamics. Because of this, the concept of courage can manifest in various ways, especially when it comes to standing up for oneself and others.

Courage in High School

1. Speaking out against bullying: Many students witness bullying but choose to remain silent. Courage involves speaking up for those who cannot defend themselves, whether that's intervening during an incident or reporting it to an adult. This act not only shows bravery but also encourages others to take a stand.

2. Defending personal beliefs: High school is often a time when students encounter diverse opinions and perspectives. Standing firm in one's beliefs, whether they relate to social issues, personal values, or cultural identity, requires courage. For instance, a student may choose to advocate for environmental protections or support a marginalized group, even when faced with opposition. All need to be heard, valued, and respected in their beliefs and sharing them to demonstrate understanding and awareness matter. Speaking with anger or judgment will just continue to divide people and further entrench them in their ideas. It's best to understand the other person before asking them to understand you.

3. Helping strangers: Sometimes, courage means stepping out of your comfort zone to extend kindness to someone you don't know. This could be as easy as inviting a new student to sit with you at lunch or helping a classmate who is struggling with coursework. Demonstrating respect for all people, regardless of their background or social standing, creates a more inclusive environment.

Courage also involves the ability to show respect for everyone around you, highlighting the importance of empathy and understanding. It means treating others, regardless of their differences, with kindness and respect. For example, encouraging a classmate struggling with their identity to express themselves freely and supporting their journey takes courage.

Additionally, actively listening to others' perspectives and acknowledging their feelings is a display of genuine empathy and courage.

It's easy to dismiss people who don't share our viewpoints, but true strength lies in engaging with them and seeking common ground.

A fundamental aspect of courage and integrity in high school is the choice to refrain from gossiping or speaking negatively about others. It may be tempting to participate in conversations that involve judgment or criticism, but intentionally ignoring this behavior is not only brave but beneficial to the school culture, as it does not endorse further discussions. You can choose not to participate, and you can gradually change the subject. Usually, most people don't have the whole story when speaking about others.

By refraining from speaking negatively about others, students foster an environment of trust and respect. When classmates see that someone refuses to engage in gossip, it encourages a positive atmosphere where everyone feels safe and valued. This, in turn, builds healthier relationships based on mutual respect. People who have nothing to say talk about others instead.

Courage in high school can take many forms, from standing up for oneself and others to fostering an environment of respect and understanding. It means acting with integrity, even when it's challenging, and treating all individuals with respect and dignity. By understanding and practicing these principles, students not only grow personally but also contribute to a more compassionate and supportive school community.

Chapter 7: The Strength of Grace

Grace meets us where we are but does not leave us where it found us.

— Anne Lamott

Grace

 What exactly is grace? How do we observe it in our daily interactions, particularly among high school students? Grace can be understood as a quality of elegance and kindness, often demonstrated through acts of compassion, humility, and respect. It becomes evident in moments when someone shows understanding toward others, accepts mistakes with poise, and offers help without expecting anything in return.

To recognize grace, look for those subtle yet powerful gestures—a student sharing notes with a classmate who's struggling, someone standing up for a friend who is being mistreated, or even a simple smile shared between peers. These instances not only uplift those involved but also create a harmonious environment in your school community. By defining grace in your terms, you'll start to notice it flourishing around you. It will be evident in your actions and can contribute to its presence, allowing others to see and follow. At its core, grace is the ability to treat others with kindness, compassion, and respect, regardless of the situation. It's not about being perfect or always saying the right thing; it's about showing a willingness to understand, empathize, and act thoughtfully.

Imagine walking through your school, where every interaction is blessed with understanding and kindness. Sounds dreamy. Grace fosters an environment where everyone feels valued and heard, turning potential conflicts into opportunities for connection. Additionally, being graceful not only reflects well on you; it also creates a ripple effect that encourages others to act with the same consideration.

Grace in High School

1. Practice empathy: Pause and think about how someone else might feel before reacting. Understanding a person's perspective can make a world of difference. Do you have a classmate who seems continuously grumpy? Perhaps they're juggling too many extracurricular activities or struggling with personal issues. A little empathy can go a long way!

2. Be mindful of your words: High school can be a hotbed for gossip and hurtful comments. Choose your words carefully, and remember that what seems like a harmless joke to you might sting deeply for someone else. Make humor a tool for connection, not division! When someone makes an unnecessary comment, you can choose to ignore it and just move on. Do not become like the person we despise to get even. An example is when someone talks rudely to you; you don't have to respond rudely in return. It's just lowering your standards. In three hours or three weeks, will it matter?

3. Offer help: Whether it's tutoring a friend struggling in math or lending your notes to someone absent, acts of kindness are at the heart of grace. Your willingness to help can create lasting bonds that extend beyond the high school hallways.

4. Apologize and forgive: Everyone makes mistakes, and grace shines particularly bright during these moments. If you mess up (and let's face it, who hasn't stepped on a few toes?), a genuine apology can heal wounds. Likewise, if someone apologizes to you, consider extending that grace by forgiving them. It matters how you respond to people because most people mirror behavior, whether they are aware of it or not. You showing grace sets the expectation for others to follow.

5. Lead by example: Just as the timeless advice of "be the change" suggests, your gracious behavior can inspire others. Show your peers that kindness is extraordinary and watch it spread like wildfire—minus the destructive part, of course! When people see grace in real life, they understand it better and will look to emulate something they are both seeking and desire to be like. It is, unfortunately, too rare, and when it is demonstrated, it reflects kindness not often seen, as we live in a world where getting back at others is the norm. Anyone who tries to get back at others when they are hurt is quite familiar; showing grace instead, and you're indeed a rare individual.

In a world that sometimes feels preoccupied with competition and superficiality, fostering grace can be a revolutionary act. So, high school student: take a step back, breathe, and embrace the power of grace. After all, in the grand tapestry of life, it's the threads of kindness and understanding that make the most beautiful patterns. Who knows? That spilled drink could lead to an unexpected friendship or a great story to tell at a reunion. Lastly, showing grace is also an act of self-preservation, as it allows you to be both kind and not get caught up in minor things that can divert you from your best path.

Chapter 8: The Habit of Gratitude

Gratitude unlocks the fullness of life.
It turns what we have into enough, and more.

— Melody Beattie

Gratitude

Gratitude is more than just saying "thank you." It's a profound recognition of the goodness in our lives and the acknowledgment of the contributions others make to our well-being. This feeling can enhance our relationships, improve our mental health, and cultivate a positive outlook on life. For high school students, understanding and expressing gratitude can build a supportive school environment and foster deeper connections with peers and teachers.

Did you know that practicing gratitude can lead to enhanced emotional and physical well-being? It helps reduce stress, increases happiness, and even promotes better sleep. By cultivating an attitude of gratitude, students can improve their overall experience in school and life. Additionally, when we express gratitude, we contribute to a culture of appreciation, which in turn encourages others to do the same.

Gratitude in High School

1. Write a thank-you note: A handwritten note can make someone's day. Whether it's a teacher who has gone above and beyond, a friend who has supported you, or a family member who has helped, taking the time to write a note shows that you value their efforts. This includes crossing guards, lunch help, the librarian, or custodial staff member. It's a very warm feeling to make someone's day.

2. Give a compliment: A sincere compliment can go a long way. It could be as easy as telling a classmate how much you appreciate their help on a group project or acknowledging a friend's achievements. Compliments promote positivity and can boost others' confidence.

3. Offer a helping hand: Sometimes, actions speak louder than words. Offering to help a bus buddy with homework, sharing lunch with someone who forgot theirs, or volunteering for a school event demonstrates gratitude for the community and its members.

4. Celebrate others' successes: Take time to acknowledge your peers' (not just your friends') achievements, whether it's a good grade, a sports win, or personal milestones. Celebrating others shows that you appreciate their hard work and encourages a supportive atmosphere.

5. Listen actively: Show gratitude by giving someone your undivided attention when they speak. Being an active listener is a powerful way to convey that you value their opinions and experiences, creating a more connected relationship. Don't have your phone in your hand or on the table. It can be viewed as a sign of not being fully present during the listening process. Give the speaker your total attention to the message. No one will say anything, but people still notice a phone, and it can be a distraction.

6. Share why you're grateful: In group discussions or casual conversations, openly share what you're grateful for. This could inspire others to do the same, leading to a chain reaction of positivity and appreciation within your circles. Instead of complaining about an unfair coach or teacher, focus on celebrating the blessings you have.

7. Say "hello" and "thank you": Every classroom you enter, walk by the teacher's desk, and make an effort to say "Hello." They may not always be approachable as they are busy, but feel free to drop it in as you walk by. They will appreciate it. On the way out, stop by and say "Thank you" while looking at them. Again, they will understand it. Make it a habit. They will both enjoy and remember your gratitude. Even more challenging is continuing to do it toward teachers who may not be your favorite, or the class that is not very interesting. That is gratitude in its purest form, as you give it with sincerity and expect nothing in return.

Incorporating gratitude into your daily life doesn't require grand gestures; small, consistent actions can yield remarkable benefits. By practicing gratitude, each student can contribute to a more positive and supportive high school environment. Take a moment to reflect on what and who you are grateful for, and start showing it in your unique way. Embrace the power of gratitude and watch it transform your relationships and experiences!

Here is a story about gratitude and how three people outside of my immediate family helped me, not because they had to, but because that's who they were. There is a difference between people who will help you because maybe that's the job or position they are in, versus somebody who has a genuine spirit about it.

Dr. Bruce Fields was my first-year basketball coach at Trinity College. I was thrilled to finally be in college and live my dream of playing collegiate basketball. Bruce was a professor at Trinity Evangelical Divinity School and was a wonderful man with a fantastic spirit for helping others and serving. He played college basketball at the University of Pennsylvania. I respected Bruce the first time I met him, which was when I was shooting baskets in the college gym. At the age of 48, he was running sprints to increase his fitness and conditioning. We had a quick introduction when he came to me and introduced himself.

As a basketball coach, he was a people person first and a basketball coach second; he blended the two roles, and I appreciated it immensely. He would treat me, talk to me, and guide me without judgment, using positive language and doing it constructively. He meant a lot to me with his guidance, and after gaining 25 pounds in my first few months of college, I weighed 175 pounds; everything on the court started to click very quickly. In the past, my strength and slender physique were always part of my struggle on the court.

Bruce guided me as I struggled with my newfound success and remaining humble. I had never had much success on the court up to that point, so my lack of maturity sometimes showed. Bruce, however, never missed a moment to teach and show me a better way, all while being kind and considerate. I remember us often having lunch and just talking about life. He shared with me that he saw a lot of himself in me when he was young. I was fortunate to have him in my life as both a coach and a friend. He later spoke at my wedding, as that is how highly I thought of him.

After completing my B.A. at Trinity College, I got married to my fantastic wife, Sheron. I also worked part-time at a Herman's World of Sporting Goods store. I worked there because it was close to my apartment, I loved sports, and the hours were good. The store manager was named Bruce Endo. He, like Bruce Fields, took the time to show me how to lead myself with courage and treat customers with a wonderful heart of service. Bruce could turn an angry customer into a fantastic way. He was a people person first and a businessman second. However, he blended both in a meaningful way, and I learned a great deal from him. It's often hard to know if you are growing or improving in life until you get to your next challenge. I had small windows of time with Bruce each day. I truly listened to what he had to say, and the wisdom began to accumulate in my ability to work with people, my confidence, and my capacity to handle whatever came my way.

There are people in your life outside your family who want to help you and invest in you. When your paths cross, you must be open-hearted and ready to listen. You might walk by them every day at school, on your team, or at your job and miss them. Be seeking and listening. You will know it when you find them, as they have a servant's heart and put people over everything else. They are investing in you and giving you the gift of time. They are a blessing.

There are people in your life outside of your family who want to help you and invest in you.

While continuing to work at Herman's World of Sporting Goods, I was interested in pursuing my Master of Science degree to help differentiate myself in the field of physical education teaching. I was hopeful that it would help me secure a job, and a good one at that. I applied to the University of Illinois at Chicago and received a letter not only accepting me but also informing me of my eligibility for an assistantship. I was ecstatic and made the appointment to interview and secure my assistantship immediately. The seeds that both Bruces had planted were starting to grow. I did well on the interview and was accepted. I attended my first class, which was only at night, and met Dr. Robin Chambers. She would be my professor the next year of my life. I was in the program for one year and had classes three nights a week.

Additionally, I had the opportunity to teach physical education at the Plato School in Chicago, a Greek school. I even got paid a small salary to teach. I was making money as a teacher. I was overwhelmed, and once again, it was about taking small steps toward significant changes; however, my confidence continued to grow. I loved everything I got to do in the program. Dr. Chambers had only a few of us in the program, and we all worked together to become better, as it was such a professional environment. I needed to have a side conversation early on with Dr. Chambers about my nervousness and my performance in the program. I did not come from a long line of academic success in the classroom. In our conversation, she explained that she was a process-based teacher, and if you put in the work, you would succeed. I can control how hard I work, so I was elated. I cannot always control how well I perform, but I am willing to do whatever it takes to do my best. I was finally achieving and feeling confident about my future, thanks to all the people who helped me along the way. Their investments were paying off for me. Dr. Chambers's mentoring, support, and process-based style were perfect for me at that time. I graduated a year later with my M.S. degree and was eager to start teaching, driven by my appreciation for my three mentors and my readiness to take on the role.

I started subbing in the area where I lived, and that went quite well. I made very favorable impressions at the places where I was a substitute teacher. I cared about those children even if I was there for only one day. I finally got a great job in a great district and was on my way. I was so blessed to have the support of my three mentors.

Here is the problematic part of this story about gratitude and why it is so important to live in the moment, embracing gratitude in every moment. Dr. Chambers moved on to Kent State University. It was not much later that I heard from a former U.I.C. classroom colleague that she had passed away suddenly. That greatly saddened me, as she invested in me and supported my personal growth. I did not get the opportunity to show her the gratitude and appreciation she deserved. Time from people is a gift, and appreciation is a form of gratitude. A lesson I still had not learned.

Time from people is a gift.

When COVID-19 became an issue in the United States and I spent a lot of time at home, I tried to respond positively. I wasn't a big user of social media back then. I set up a Facebook account and began searching for some of the outstanding students from my teaching past, as well as for both Bruces. I found many opportunities to reconnect with former students, which I valued. When I went looking for the two men who were my mentors, much to my heartbreak, they had both passed away. To this day, I deeply regret the lack of gratitude I failed to show them—a painful and profound lesson that remains with me.

Live with courage and show gratitude to the people who help and hold you accountable. They don't have to invest in you, but they do, which is a powerful act of caring. Many people in the cemetery believed they had more time. I want you to learn from my mistake, one I learned the hard way and still live with. Some people find my zealous gratitude a little too much at times, but I never want to repeat the lesson I just shared with you.

You have read small ways to practice all these attitudes and skills. These are just a few ideas, as there are many more. If you start small and make it a small habit, it will take root in you and grow. That is just who you will become, and you will be that way without thinking about it. That is the path to greatness. Realize that any mistakes you make are life lessons that, if you learn from them, will serve you. You can change and develop your attitude into a more positive one, day by day, through small acts of kindness that accumulate over time. You just have to start, and today is that day. An expression says, "The best time to plant a tree was 20 years ago; the second-best time is today."

If you're pursuing this type of greatness, consider that you must embrace daily, reflect on, and search your heart and mind to build these qualities into the fabric of who you are. Performing small daily acts often promotes awareness and a positive habit and mindset. Do not seek answers, be the answer. The strength to show these qualities will allow you to shine humbly. This is a constant pursuit that will grow within you and mature as you do, if you continually practice all the areas.

If it does not happen in you, it cannot happen through you.
— Attributed to James Hollis

Pursue greatness and enhance your character and your daily life quality for you and others. When will you start? Living with greatness requires more than just action; it also requires deep self-reflection. In the next chapter, we'll ask the challenging questions that help you look beyond the surface.

One day or day one. You decide.

— Attributed to Paulo Coelho

Your One-Degree Shift

- Write one thank-you note this week to a teacher, family member, or friend who helped you.

- For the next two days, make a point to say "thank you" to the cafeteria staff or a custodian at school.

Chapter 9: Your Character Is Showing

Character is like a tree, and reputation like its shadow. The shadow is what we think of it; the tree is the real thing.

— Abraham Lincoln

It is not often, but I occasionally see people who treat those with authority with great respect, while they treat others who have little authority over them poorly. An example I have seen is in the cafeteria, where an associate or teacher's aide asks a student to do something or not do something, and the person refuses or is hesitant to comply. The staff member asks the person at the lunch table to please dispose of all the food wrappers on the table. An individual currently eating at the same table says the wrappers on the table are not theirs. This may or may not be true. But that is not the point; the point is, is it that difficult to be helpful and support all school staff by assisting them with small tasks in the cafeteria? The answer is no, it's not.

The highest level of helpfulness would be to clean it up, even if it's not yours, because that is who you are and how you think. You are demonstrating character. Your mindset is that I am always looking to be helpful. The selfless mindset is that if someone asks you to help, you would simply answer, "Sure, I can do that." The selfish mindset is to respond in a way that says, "That is not mine," which brings no resolution to the issue at hand. That is a small example of how you treat others who have no authority over you. I have seen the selfish mindset more often than I care to remember. I hope that those with selfish mindsets outgrow them, as that attitude will cost them as they grow up. The consequences of a disrespectful mindset can be far-reaching, affecting not only your relationships but also your personal growth and development. As you move through your day, make sure to treat everyone with the best approach, because that is who you are working to be. Their position or title does not determine the amount of respect and cooperation you will show them. The actual test of your maturity and respect is that you treat everyone with respect, even if they don't deserve it.

Here is a story to illustrate the principles.

There's a famous legend about how Henry Ford used a simple dinner to find the right person for a major job.

As the story goes, Ford had narrowed down the search to two excellent candidates. On paper, they were identical—perfect grades, stellar qualifications, and impressive ambition. Unable to separate them, Ford invited both to a restaurant for an informal dinner interview.

Throughout the meal, Ford watched them closely. He noticed two seemingly small details that told him everything he needed to know. First, when their food arrived, one candidate immediately reached for the salt shaker and seasoned his food before taking a single bite. The other candidate tasted his food first, considered it for a moment, and then decided it needed nothing.

Second, Ford observed how each man treated the waitstaff. The candidate who salted his food mindlessly was dismissive, barely acknowledging the server. The other was polite, making eye contact and saying "please" and "thank you."

At the end of the meal, Ford had made his decision. He offered the job to the second candidate—the one who tasted his food first and treated the server with respect.

When the rejected candidate asked why, Ford explained his reasoning. He said the man who salted his food without tasting it showed a willingness to make assumptions without first gathering information. More importantly, the man who was rude to the server revealed that he only respected people he thought could help him.

The candidate he hired, however, had demonstrated curiosity, humility, and consistent character. He didn't assume the food needed fixing, and he treated everyone with dignity, not just the person in power. Ford wasn't just hiring a resume; he was hiring a person of integrity.

That dinner was Henry Ford's version of a character test. You face similar tests every day—not in a job interview, but in how you treat a substitute teacher, the cafeteria staff, or a new student who looks lost. Your character is always on display, especially when you think no one is watching.

Watch out for people who have a situational value system, who can turn the charm on and off depending on the status of the person they are interacting with. Be especially wary of those who are rude to people perceived to be in subordinate roles.

— Bill Swanson

Your One-Degree Shift

- The next time you're in the cafeteria or a restaurant, make eye contact with the staff, say "please" and "thank you," and leave your space cleaner than you found it.

- The next time you have a substitute teacher, be the first person to offer help or to quiet down a disruptive group.

Chapter 10: Respect versus Like

Character—the willingness to accept responsibility for one's own life—is the source from which self-respect springs.

— Joan Didion

When I was young, I had never heard of the distinction between liking someone and respecting them. After some self-reflection, I can say that I pursued "like" as a high schooler and never considered respect as an option. I worked hard to be "liked" by others. The pursuit of being liked is both draining and challenging, as it requires acting in a way that you think others might want you to be, to try to fit in. It often left me feeling like I was on the outside looking in socially. I shared this feeling in Chapter 1; I was popular, but I never felt like I fit in. It was a pretty painful pursuit. Then, when I was about 24 years old, I heard a friend of mine speak about a talk he had attended, given by former basketball great Doug Collins, on the difference between liking and respecting, and how it had stuck with him. He later shared the concept with me. It was like a bolt of lightning hit me. It stuck, and from that moment on, I was a different person walking a different path. People want to be liked, but I

don't compromise on the value of being
respected first.

I focused on respect first and like second.

— Attributed to Mike Krzyzewski

I started developing my standards and
started reading more about the subject and
performance. By "performance," I mean the way
I present myself to the world, the actions taken,
and the decisions made. Things began to click
for me, and I felt like a new person, aiming for
respect for who I am and how I operate. I
continue to develop and refine my standards
today. I also have standards for how I treat

people. I focus on showing people respect, whether they deserve it or not.

Being liked is a tough road, and when you're young, it seems the most logical way to navigate as you try to find a place where you fit in. Being liked is also subjective, and the line of being liked can shift constantly, causing you to continually adapt and change to fit in. It becomes a draining and never-ending pursuit to catch up and stay in the group. Operating that way often left me feeling lonely and confused, and it felt like a dog chasing its tail. No matter how fast or hard you chase being liked, you will never catch up to or arrive at it.

I want people to like me, but I will not compromise to be liked. Being liked usually involves an emotional connection, which is how you feel, a subjective value that may not necessarily include respect. Being respected entails admiration based on integrity, wisdom, and objectivity, which reflects a person's dignity and value. Feeling respected is a more comfortable daily experience that allows you to walk with consistency, without worrying about what others are thinking. That does not mean you don't care how they feel; you certainly still care how they feel, but in the long run, it's about respect and standing tall.

Pursuing being liked is a never-ending chase. I have walked on both paths; the respect path is both rewarding and consistent. Being respected for having your standards is what you're seeking; being liked and changing all the time to fit into a group or to belong are external values that keep changing. Trying to be liked often costs me self-respect at times, and the saying goes, if it costs you self-respect, it's too expensive.

Chapter 11: How You Do Anything Is How You Do Everything

Do the best you can until you know better.
Then, when you know better, do better.

— Maya Angelou

The author Martha Beck is credited with the saying, "How you do anything is how you do everything." It's a powerful idea to ponder. Is it true for you? The concept focuses on the quality of who you want to be and challenges you to maintain one high standard for everything you're a part of, rather than a separate set of expectations for what you deem essential versus unimportant. This raises a critical question: Do the small things matter as much as the big ones? If your answer is "no," it allows you to justify not doing your best on tasks you consider less necessary. This creates two sets of standards: a high one for the 'important' things and a lower one for everything else. But what if you're wrong about what's essential? As we discussed earlier, significant moments in life are often disguised as small, everyday situations. If you choose not to do your best on the "small things," you may just miss your life-changing moment.   I have adopted the mantra, "How you do anything is how you do everything." I focus on what I can control, and I know that if I am involved in something, I will do a great job. I do this because that is the single standard I hold myself to in everything I do.

Chapter 12: The Blind Benefits of Doing Your Best

Success is peace of mind, which is a direct result of self-satisfaction in knowing you did your best to become the best that you are capable of becoming.

— John Wooden

When I was first looking for a job at the age of 24, I started substitute-teaching in a few different school districts. On my first day as a substitute, I was assigned to a junior high school. The administration told me I would be teaching a drafting class for the day. I had a drafting class  in junior high, but I wasn't good enough to lead instruction. The drafting class introduces students to the fundamental principles of drawing and design. Today's computers have rendered this class obsolete. The teacher set up a plan where students would know what to do for the day, and I would ensure attendance was taken. Then, I would support them and keep them focused during the 45-minute class. After about 10 minutes into the very first class, six boys decided they had had enough focus time and started goofing around by being loud and disruptive. The rest of the class struggled to continue with the work due to the distractions they were causing. I asked them nicely multiple times to stop and please get back on track.

As a new teacher, I knew I would be overwhelmed if I didn't set boundaries quickly. I took a high-risk approach. I sent another student to the office and instructed them to find an available administrator and have them come to our class. The student left and returned minutes later. About five more minutes passed with the students remaining uncooperative when an administrator opened the classroom door and looked in. He made eye contact with me and asked me to step out into the hallway. I was unsure how this was going to go, as I thought I might appear as someone unable to control the classroom and might seem incompetent.

I shared my name and what I was doing with him, as well as how the six boys had continually disregarded my straightforward and fair requests for more cooperation. He said to me, "Can you send the six boys in the hallway and come out with them?" I responded with a nod and went into the classroom, and sent the six boys out into the hallway. The gentleman then shared with the boys, "I hear you boys are not being helpful to our substitute, who has asked you many times to be more cooperative. Is this true?" They all nodded. Then he said, "You spread the word if I have to come down to any other classes today in drafting with our substitute teacher; there will be consequences." The boys all nodded again and returned to the classroom. He then said to me, "Can you please stop by my office after school when you are done?" I said, "Yes," and was a little nervous until the end of the day. When the final bell rang, I went down to his office and found out that he was the assistant principal. He shared how much he appreciated my stepping up and expecting the best from students at school. I expressed my appreciation for his support and shared that every school day is essential and counts in a student's development. Then, I briefly recounted my story and informed him that I was seeking a teaching position for the next school year. I finished up and said, "Thank you," and I was on my way home soon after. I never saw that man again in my time subbing in that district for the rest of the school year.

As the school year came to a close and summer approached, I was still seeking a teaching job. I applied for a job in the very district where I had frequently subbed, as well as in many other districts where I had also subbed. As it turned out, that administrator had just been promoted to principal at another school in the district that had an opening for a part-time teaching position. Well, I got the job over the summer because of that moment in the drafting class. He remembered me and was impressed with my level of caring, especially as a substitute teacher. Mark soon became a mentor of mine as a young teacher, despite going on to full-time work at a different school the following year. I worked in faith, knowing that while subbing and doing my best, I hoped to make a difference. As a substitute with no guarantees of anything happening employment-wise, it turned out that doing the right thing all the time paid off. It came full circle: my effort and commitment served me even when I didn't see or know it.

This is an example of how being caring and doing your best will come back to help you. Had I not cared, I would not have gotten a great job and had an outstanding career. I have also cared many times with nothing materializing, but I did it for the sake of doing my best in helping others. Interestingly, a moment can occur, and you may not even recognize it. It could be happening to you, too; you just don't know when. So, there are no timeouts for doing your best; someone is always watching, and somewhere, sometime, it could change your life. Always be vigilant and fully present. You never know who is observing.

Section B: Managing Your Inner World

In the last section, we laid the groundwork by defining the core virtues of a life that defies average—honor, kindness, courage, and respect. But knowing who to be is only half the battle. Now, we turn inward to answer the question of how. The following chapters are about managing your inner world, providing you with the tools to build the confidence, discipline, and focus needed to embody those character traits every day.

Chapter 13: How Do You Build Confidence?

You gain strength, courage, and confidence by every experience in which you really stop to look fear in the face. You must do the thing you think you cannot do.

— Eleanor Roosevelt

Confidence is both earned and developed over time. We need to grow by working in a struggle zone, combined with deliberate practice. This will significantly improve confidence through dedicated hours of committed time to develop the skills we want to excel in, allowing us to perform them at a high level when needed. How we use our time is one of the most significant variables in growing our confidence.

An example of time invested is something that I advise all my basketball players: If they struggle with dribbling a basketball well in high school, it's their responsibility. They haven't put in enough time to improve their dribbling skills. They do have 10 to 15 minutes a day to go and dribble two basketballs in their garage or basement in a challenging way. They need to perform with deliberate practice in a way that allows them to make mistakes and feel just beyond comfortable, but not to a level where they can't grasp the basics or improve. Do they have the daily desire and the discipline to do it each day? Quite often, it's a wish they had in a basketball moment, but not a significant focus when practice is over. They would make it a priority if they genuinely wanted to improve and grow their confidence in that skill. That is true of almost everyone. We want things, but don't put in the time to continually progress in the things we say we want. Most of the time, the player's answer is no, as it was just a fleeting wish.

When we discuss confidence, we need to focus on what we do to cultivate it in the areas where we want to feel it. Everyone, at all levels and in every field, has doubts, struggles, and challenges in various areas of life. Realize you're not alone.

Remember, even I, as a coach, have moments of doubt. When I lack confidence, I remind myself, "Focus on what I can control," and repeat this mantra out loud often in challenging moments. It helps me focus on my controllables, which in turn restores my confidence in moments when I lack it or it is teetering. I often find myself worrying about things I cannot control, which distracts me from the present moment and wastes my mental energy. Additionally, my focus tends to get lost very quickly, which in turn increases stress. However, this is self-inflicted, mainly when I start to think about things I cannot control. We have already discussed how to talk to ourselves. That is also an essential part of the confidence equation. Go back and read that again if you need a refresher. Remember, your self-talk is a powerful tool in building your confidence. Use it to empower yourself and take control of your journey, increasing your confidence.

As you can see, many aspects contribute to your confidence. You should reread this section to identify what you're doing well and where you need to focus more attention. Realize that this takes time, but if you focus on it and work in a zone where the line is just over being comfortable, you'll accelerate your growth, and right behind that is your growing confidence. The same principle applies to math, science, literature, and every other field. Time on task will help you grow and increase your ever-growing confidence. Always realize everyone starts with little to no confidence. They must develop and grow it over time. Some people are very confident, but they know they have put in the time, and now their confidence serves them well in challenging situations. You only have a limited amount of time each day. You get 86,400 seconds per day, so allocate 1,200 seconds daily to a skill you want to master. Do it seven days a week, whether you feel like it or not. So, whatever your priorities are, use your time intentionally to improve each day. If your confidence is not growing, it's time to reevaluate how you are using your time and adjust your priorities accordingly.

Remember, we all start from the same place of low confidence, and it's the path toward growth that matters. You have a choice on how to use your time; use it wisely.

Your One-Degree Shift

- Spend 10 minutes today deliberately practicing a skill you want to improve—like dribbling a basketball, practicing a math problem, or drawing.

- Look in the mirror and say one positive, encouraging thing to yourself out loud.

Chapter 14: Motivation Is the Spark, Discipline Is the Engine

*You don't have to be motivated every day.
You just have to be disciplined.*

— Attributed to Jocko Willink

A student recently asked me, "Hey, coach, what is your pump-up jam?" My answer was that I don't really have one anymore. When I was younger, I'd listen to AC/DC before a game, but the pump-up was always temporary. Once the game started, that external energy was gone.

This is the perfect picture of motivation. It's the spark or initial energy that gets you started. It's the reason you decide to go on a diet, start a new workout, or finally pick up a book. But that spark doesn't last. A notable example is the New Year's resolution. On January 1st, motivation is high, and gyms are packed. By the second Friday of the month—often referred to as "Quitter's Day"—most people have already abandoned their goals because the initial excitement has faded and they haven't seen immediate results.

If motivation is the spark, then discipline is the engine that keeps you going long after the spark is gone. Most people hear the word "discipline" and think of punishment.

I want you to see it differently. Discipline is a form of self-respect that sets you free. It's not a chore; it's the commitment to making choices that serve your future self.

This is where the difference between having intentions and being intentional comes in. An intention is a wish: "I meant to clean my room," or "I'll call you tomorrow." It has no real power. Being intentional is a plan: "I will clean my room on Saturday at 10 a.m.," or "I will call you on Tuesday at 4 p.m." Being intentional is the practical application of discipline. You are scheduling your actions, making them real, and holding yourself accountable.

When you show this level of discipline—at home, in the classroom, with your friends—you earn trust and freedom. You prove you're dependable. The benefits compound over time. The small, disciplined choice to read 15 pages a day will make you a different person in a year. Deciding to resist soda today can help transform your health within a decade. Consistency wins.

So, when you feel excited and motivated, use that spark to create a plan. But on all the other days when you don't feel like it, rely on your discipline to power the engine. Remember, your feelings aren't your action plan—your discipline is. It's the key that unlocks your long-term success.

Chapter 15: Sharpening the Saw: The Need for "Me Time"

Give me six hours to chop down a tree, and I will spend the first four sharpening the axe.

— Anonymous

At this point in my life, I have learned something that we all nod in agreement to when we hear it, but don't do it because we are just too busy. Well, being busy is easy; being productive is harder. I have learned to schedule some time to recharge. It's something that I build into the first part of my day. I need it. When I skip it, I'm not at my best, and my mindset changes. I have found that very early in the morning is an excellent time for me, which is why I typically go to bed between 9:00 and 9:30 p.m. every night. While some people want to stay up late, that can ruin the next day. An early bedtime allows me to wake up energized and makes my feelings much more predictable.

My day typically starts after I have a morning glass of tea or water. I will then go on a 6- to 10-mile walk three to four times per week, regardless of the outside conditions. I realize the weather is only temporary, so I just take precautions, even in rain or freezing temperatures. If I skip it, I'll feel it, and it could lead to another missed day, which can snowball into many more. I refuse to let that happen. When I go on my walks, I don't bring music; I walk alone to appreciate nature, which allows me to clear my mind and focus on the people I care about. Besides the mental and spiritual benefits, I also push my pace to about 15:30 per mile, which is a great way to improve my overall fitness.

While walking is my method, there are many other ways to recharge. I sometimes enjoy rucking, which is walking with a weighted backpack. Other powerful ways to find "me time" include journaling, reading, listening to calming music, and even taking a 1-hour nap. A nap is a great way to rest, even if you don't fall asleep; however, it's essential to set an alarm to avoid disrupting your nighttime sleep cycle.

I can hear some of you saying, "I don't have time." Most days, you do. You simply need to adjust your priorities, because what you water grows. You need to water yourself constantly. Spending time recharging with positive "me time" that helps you grow and reflect is exceptionally valuable. Try it for two weeks and start small. Be intentional about when you plan to do it; otherwise, you won't. Remember, you and the world deserve the best version of you! Control your well-being and prioritize self-care.

Sharpening the Saw

There's an old parable that perfectly illustrates the need to recharge.

Two woodcutters decided to see who could chop the most wood in a single day. The first, driven by pure determination, began chopping and didn't stop, barely taking a break. He worked relentlessly from sunrise to sunset.

The second woodcutter worked differently. He would chop intensely for about an hour, then stop for a full 15 minutes. The first woodcutter could hear the silence from across the forest and smirked, thinking his competitor's lack of stamina would guarantee his victory. This pattern continued all day: one hour of chopping, followed by 15 minutes of silence.

When they measured their piles of wood at the end of the day, everyone was surprised to see that the second woodcutter—the one who took regular breaks—had chopped significantly more.

"How is this possible?" the first woodcutter asked, exhausted and confused. "I heard you stop working every single hour!"

The second woodcutter smiled and replied, "Yes, but while you kept chopping with a dulling blade, I was using that time to sharpen my saw."

The lesson is clear: non-stop effort isn't always the most effective. Actual productivity requires taking the time to rest, recharge, and refine your tools—whether that tool is a saw or your own mind. Working smart will always beat working hard.

Chapter 16: Are You in Control of Your Phone, or Is It Controlling You?

You have power over your mind—not outside events. Realize this, and you will find strength.

— Marcus Aurelius

Do you ever stop to consider the true cost of your phone usage? When you look back on hours spent scrolling, what did you really gain? More often than not, the price is your time—time that could have been spent with people you value or on things that truly matter. You might feel like you can't help yourself, that the device just keeps you hooked. That feeling is intentional. **Let's be real**; your phone is designed by geniuses to do precisely that.

So why do we constantly fall for it? It comes down to two powerful forces. The first is dopamine, the brain's "feel-good" neurotransmitter. Every message, like, or notification provides a small hit of this chemical, making you want to return to the source for more. This reward cycle is what

 makes your phone so addictive. On average, people check their phones 84 times a

day—roughly every 12 minutes. That isn't just a habit; it's a dependency. The second force is algorithms, which are engineered to capture your attention by personalizing your feed based on your viewing history. The more you watch, the better the algorithm gets at feeding you content you can't resist.

Understanding that your phone is designed to be addictive helps reveal its hidden costs. The most obvious price is paid in time—lost hours for studying, reading, connecting with family, or simply being present with friends. But the toll is more profound than that. Studies consistently link excessive phone use to increased anxiety, depression, stress, sleep issues, and social withdrawal. While no one plans for these consequences, they are the inevitable outcome of the habit.

The costs continue to accumulate, often in ways we don't immediately notice: decreased attention span, lower academic performance, and a waning interest in real-world hobbies.

This doesn't even touch on the devastating impact of online bullying, which I have witnessed too many times in my career. The final, crucial question, then, is a personal one. What is your phone truly costing *you*? You may feel like the answer is "nothing," but the price may already be higher than you realize. Check your screen time stats, and be honest with yourself about where the hours are really going.

Your One-Degree Shift

- Check your phone's screen time report. Pick one app you want to spend less time on.

- Tonight, put your phone away for a full 30 minutes before you plan to go to sleep.

Chapter 17: Consider Your Influences

You must constantly stand guard at the door of your mind, and you alone decide what thoughts and beliefs you let into your life.

— Jim Rohn

Do you ever consider what you read, watch, and talk about, and how it's influencing you? Does that matter? Everything matters, so do you try to control or manage the influences that affect you and the people you surround yourself with? It affects your choices and how you see the world. It can and will affect personal growth, taking it in either direction.

Consider filtering your influences as you shape your standards so that you're not negatively affected by poor input. Just as you're what you eat, you're what you're influenced by. Although you may not feel the effects immediately, we know that they will accumulate over time. Just as a person trying to eat well to improve their health and wellness would be moving away from their goal by cheating on their diet, this also applies to your best version of yourself if you don't filter what you consume through your phone, social media, TV, and friends. It slows your progress and takes you off your best path.

Would it not be the same if what influences you becomes part of you, and thus can move you in the wrong direction from who you want to be? Traveling down the wrong path begins with a first step. I realize people are curious by nature, so we cannot let what we watch, read, or talk about deter us from our path.

In his book, *What to Say When You Talk to Your Self,* author Shad Helmstetter writes: "Whatever you put into your mind, in one way or another, is what you will get back, in one way or another." That is a compelling thought. Protect what goes into your mind, and guard what influences you so you don't drift from the best version of you.

Chapter 18: A Thought on Remembering

Your mind is for having ideas, not holding them.

— David Allen

Have you ever considered how many thoughts you have in a day? When I ask students this question, most say they have no idea, and I would have felt the same way at that age. Many people don't even think about it. However, it's essential to remember that struggling with memory and organization is a common challenge, not a personal failure. Recognizing the sheer volume of thoughts you experience can help improve your self-esteem and often motivate you to act. A recent study suggests that the average person has around 6,200 thoughts per day. This finding was based on research using fMRI brain imaging and "thought worms" to track thought transitions. The study, published in the journal Nature Communications, was conducted by researchers at Queen's University in Canada [Tseng, J., Poppenk, J. Brain meta-state transitions demarcate thoughts across task contexts exposing the mental noise of trait neuroticism.

Nat Commun 11, 3480 (2020). https://doi.org/10.1038/s41467-020-17255-9].

Struggling with memory and organization is a common challenge, not a personal failure.

As you can see, you have many thoughts per day. You average around 6.5 thoughts per minute. Your brain is jam-packed with thinking. You might ask yourself, "If I think so much, why can't I remember something simple, like my math homework?" Think of your mind like Grand Central Station. With over 6,000 "passengers" (thoughts) rushing through every day, trying to hold onto one specific piece of information is like trying to keep track of a single suitcase in the middle of a crowd. It's not a failure of memory; it's a matter of logistics. **Writing something down** is like putting that suitcase in a secure locker. It takes the pressure off your brain to remember it.

While your brain may be active with thoughts, you might still struggle to remember certain things. Everyone is different, so if memory is a challenge for you, start by developing an easy method to create lists and keep track of your homework, due dates, and upcoming tests and quizzes. The sooner you begin organizing your tasks, the better you will feel and the more successful you will become.

As an executive functioning coach, I encourage students to write things down at the end of each class in a way that takes less than 30 seconds to complete. Remember, if it's easy to do, it's also easy not to do. Don't plan to write it down later during lunch or at the end of the day; make it a habit to do it right after each class. You can even place a sticky note on the inside of your computer as a reminder.

In high school, you have a lot on your mind—not just thoughts, but also learning and memory challenges, as well as personal development. Keep moving forward, be kind to yourself, and continue to discover what works best for you. This path of self-discovery and finding effective strategies is one of personal growth and empowerment. You will find your way, but, like Thomas Edison with the light bulb, it may take several tries. Thomas Edison reportedly tried between 1,000 and 6,000 filaments in his work to create a light bulb. I am sure it will not take you that long to find the best plan for you.

I share more ideas about strategies in the executive functioning section in Chapter 90.

Chapter 19: Your Brain Is Your Universe

A mind that is stretched by a new experience can never go back to its old dimensions.

— Oliver Wendell Holmes Jr.

I remember (and continue to hear to this day) students asking, "When am I ever going to use this?" I believe that sometimes students are right; they may never use what they're learning, but that doesn't make it not worth knowing. Just like a universe, your brain is always

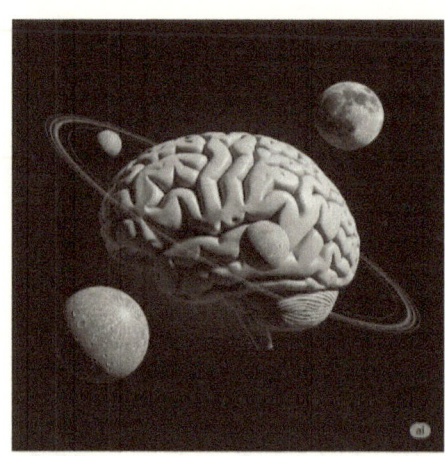

constantly growing, changing, and expanding. This is called neuroplasticity, a genuine scientific concept that explains how your brain forms new connections and grows neurons throughout life, even as you age in your later years. As you explore its vastness, you'll never know its boundaries, and the joy of continuously discovering your future and its potential is exhilarating. What if our prior space programs had focused solely on exploring the moon and

Mercury, given that Mercury is the planet that is most consistently closest to Earth?

We will never be able to go to the far, far away planets, so let's not even learn about them. We will never use them. Doesn't that sound familiar? We're deciding not to study them now, so let's not bother with them in the future. It is humankind's mission to continue exploring, because one never knows where any of this development could lead humanity, both now and in the future. A discovery in the universe today could change everything and help us gain a deeper understanding of ourselves, which in turn could alter our future.

The parallel is also true of your universe, which I am referring to as your brain. You need to keep expanding and exploring all of it so that it can grow, change, and you can continue to help it grow. One day, it will serve you well, having developed and studied all aspects, and learned for the sake of learning, not just "do you think we will ever use this stuff someday?"

Keep your brain expanding and refrain from judging what you're learning, as this helps you develop and learn to think in different ways. And just like our space exploration going in every direction for the benefit of humanity, you keep expanding in every direction to benefit you and your potential development.

Chapter 20: Failure Doesn't Exist—Only Lessons

I never lose. I either win or learn.

— Attributed to Nelson Mandela

I often ask students what they have ever failed at in their lives. The answer is always given in regard to a test or quiz. Why is that? Because it makes up a large part of their current world. I ask them to think even bigger, and here's why: If they learned something from getting a poor grade, then they did not fail the quiz or the test. You could be legalistic and say, "Yes, they still failed it," but that is not my point. Suppose they learned something about the process. I suggest they improve their preparation or allocate more time for tasks that require their attention. So, they did not fail in the big world because they improved their knowledge and could take action to create a better outcome for themselves the next time.

In an interview with the late great Kobe Bryant, the interviewer asked a question about how Kobe handled failure as a professional athlete. To paraphrase Kobe's response, "There is no such thing as failure in life as long as you don't quit, and I am not a quitter. People invented the concept of failure. I learn from my mistakes, so I don't think failure exists." His mindset was always to use what happened as a means to move forward and never stop improving (MykChiz, KOBE BRYANT - "FAILURE DOESNT [sic] EXIST," posted on December 27, 2017, YouTube video, https://www.youtube.com/watch?v=js8OfeEL4jI).

This approach is very liberating and does not make us feel like failures. It also helps our self-talk become and stay positive, as mistakes and struggles should be viewed as opportunities for growth. I know many people use the term "failure," and I am never going to stop them, but I will flip the switch in my brain and ask, "What did I learn from that situation?" It's a positive reflection of a growth mindset. So, if you don't do well on something, use it as an opportunity to reflect upon it and ask yourself, "What did I learn for next time?" Embrace a growth mindset, and you will find that every challenge is an opportunity for growth.

Chapter 21: There Are No Bad Days, Just Bad Moments

It's not the situation, but whether we react negatively or positively to the situation that is important.

— Zig Ziglar

I hear this expression, and I sometimes struggle with it: 95 percent of the time, there are no bad days, just bad moments. An argument, a disagreement, a test we study hard for, a friend talking behind your back, a coach not playing you in a game, a project not going as planned, a job rejection, and more—these are examples of difficult moments. We often get into a mindset when we ask someone, "How is your day?" or "How was your day?" that there are only two choices: good or bad. We have discussed all the blessings we have, and yet we often quickly forget them when we have a bad moment. I would encourage you to try to remember the blessings you have in a bad moment; it keeps things in perspective of what "bad" really is. It is with great care and sensitivity that I express my belief that we can indeed have bad days, but very few in a lifetime. A bad day is the loss of a loved one, a life-altering medical diagnosis, or losing a family pet. Nothing hurts more in life than losing someone you loved and cared about, someone who may have made a difference in your life. You will miss that person, and that often hurts in the worst way.

Losing someone, whether it was before what we think their time should have been on this planet or later in their life, even if they had a great life and it was their time, just hurts. Those emotions are overwhelming, and the heaviness of the loss allows for an actual bad day. Usually, this is followed by some very challenging days, which can last for a considerable time as we grieve. The second idea behind what I would consider a bad day is when we receive life-altering news that changes our lives for the worse. Nobody ever wishes to hear they have cancer. Even writing this paragraph is emotional for me because I think about the people I have loved and lost to cancer and other conditions, and it just hurts and makes my eyes well up. Reflecting on loss is a profoundly difficult moment that can last a long time and resurface unexpectedly, often without warning.

I understand those losses, and usually we ask, "Why?" For reasons like this, we can have a bad day. Otherwise, we have bad moments. I want to explore how we sometimes frame a bad moment. When you get home and someone asks you a standard school question, like "Do you have homework?" you may have a lot of homework that day. What about when a parent drives home from work and gets stuck in traffic? As a commuter, you should expect traffic delays, but it can still be challenging for you. You plan a fun day outside, but it's raining. While these are disappointments, how can we not expect them to be possible and sometimes happen? Keep an open mind about all the things that can happen in your life, but that doesn't mean you have to like them all. However, they are an integral part of our lives. The idea is not to complain, as you know, we may have a lot of homework, a slow commute, or get rained out. These are common occurrences in the world, so keep going and understand that they are likely to happen.

Your response indicates whether you know how to focus on what you can control and what is beyond your control. Concentrating on what is out of our control can easily make a day seem bad and frustrating, but in reality, you have no power; however, you do have control over your response. One practical tip for reframing bad moments is to practice gratitude. When faced with disappointment, take a moment to think about the things you're grateful for. An attitude like this can help shift your perspective and turn a bad moment into a good one.

Chapter 22: What If Your Biggest Fears Aren't Real?

Too many of us are not living our dreams because we are living our fears.

— Les Brown

When we observe people thriving in significant moments, whether in sports or other performances, it most often stems from their mindset. They think differently from those who see and accept failure or succumb to peer pressure. They know the moment before they arrive that they are ready to do their best, knowing it may not work out, but still willing to give it a try. Failure is typically defined as a moment when things don't unfold as planned. What if we reframed failure as merely a learning experience? Instead of being an endpoint, it can be viewed as part of the growth process of improvement. To achieve this, we must stop listening to outside voices and adopt a growth mindset that enables us to learn, progress, and develop our voice from within, creating a willingness to step into those moments of great challenge in a game or situation. This perspective offers a healthier approach to navigating critical moments. Rather than viewing a failure as a setback, we could see it as mistakes made that offer lessons for future opportunities. We learn from them and move on.

Similarly, consider a business that is failing and ultimately closes its doors. That is upsetting and disappointing, but understanding what went wrong and why can provide valuable insights for future business ventures. Those lessons learned can accompany you as you move forward. Turning setbacks into growth moments will serve you in the future. There are no permanent labels. They are just a moment in time when you were willing to step up and try, and it did not go your way. So, learn from it and move on. Thus, failure can exist if you allow it to, depending on how you choose to interpret your past experiences.

Peer pressure operates under a similar concept but occurs within a group context. You may feel peer pressure, but that doesn't mean it is inherently real. The belief that you must conform to the group's expectations to belong can create internal pressure.

The sooner you start setting your own standards, the sooner you can leave peer pressure behind.

When walking your path, peer pressure may feel less impactful because you're moving in a direction that aligns with your goals. However, if you're straying from your path to follow or be in the group, then peer pressure can feel very real, as the group's influence appears stronger than your path trajectory. This means you're willing to compromise to fit in, and that can be very expensive in terms of self-respect, dignity, character, and more.

Interestingly, the feeling of peer pressure can often diminish with maturity. I have witnessed adults yielding to perceived peer pressure, while I have also seen young children who are already adept at resisting it. The sooner you start focusing on thinking differently and setting your standards, the sooner you can leave behind the words and feelings of failure and peer pressure.

Chapter 23: You Are Your Most Significant Investment

The most important investment you can make is in yourself.

— Warren Buffett

You have to look at yourself as a bank and make deposits each day that will grow for you over time. You are your biggest investor in who you will become. Suppose you invest a great deal in yourself by working hard in the classroom, being involved in clubs, and participating in other extracurricular activities, such as reading, exercising, and maintaining a healthy diet. In this case, you're not only growing as an individual but also preparing for future experiences that will ultimately help you succeed and live the quality of life you're seeking. Someday, when you apply for a job and have volunteer service experiences, it will help you because you have developed skills working with people. It all stacks up as you invest in yourself. Others can help, support, and walk with you, but you need to drive the investment opportunities for yourself. It's that simple. People who are hiring at any company will compare you to others who are also applying for the same job. Your experience and self-investment will speak for you as you will only be there in name and on paper, or a resume. Invest early and often, and set yourself apart from others as your hard work and commitment speak for themselves. Remember, the earlier you start, the more you can achieve and the greater investment you can make in yourself. No action equals no investment.

Chapter 24: "I Didn't Have Time"

Dost thou love life? Then do not squander time,
for that is the stuff life is made of.

— Benjamin Franklin

Sometimes we fail to plan well and run out of time with things we intended to do. It happens. What you need to be aware of is that when you repeatedly express running out of time to someone, it will most likely be received as if they are not a priority. Let's be real; when they consistently hear you say you don't have time, you are saying you don't  have time for them. Taking it one step further, "I didn't make time for you" is the absolute truth. We prioritize our time by what needs to be done and what we want to do. Time is a precious gift, and giving it to people shows their importance to you. "I didn't have time" can mean they are not a priority, and that can hurt their feelings and send a message that they are not very important to you. If I tell someone I will do something, I will. I will stay up late, get up early, and take a shorter lunch, because my words mean that much to me. When I share or say something to someone, it's my gold standard, and I hold it in high value. So be careful when you tell someone you don't have time; they may take it as a sign that they are not important, because what we value, we give our time to. Be wise and make your words both trustworthy and as valuable as gold.

Section C: Your Impact on Others

Mastering your inner world is the first step, but the true test of your growth is how it shows up in your interactions. Having explored the internal habits for building discipline and focus, it's time to shift our attention outward. The following chapters will explore how your mindset directly affects your relationships and community. After all, defying average isn't just about changing yourself; it's about making a positive impact on the lives of those around you.

Chapter 25: What If Everyone Were You?

Self-reflection is the school of wisdom.

— Baltasar Gracian

Think about it for a second: What if everyone behaved the way you currently do in class? What would it look like? This could go in two different directions. If you're being a distraction, and if everyone were mirroring your choice in attitude and class contribution, would you find yourself helpful? On the other hand, if you're engaged, focused, and contributing in class, are you being helpful? Sometimes students look at themselves and think they are doing fine, but they have not yet considered this viewpoint. If everyone were doing what you were, what would it look like? To answer the question, do not be yourself; instead, think of yourself as if you were the trendsetter. Your answer should guide you in how you represent yourself and help you determine whether you're making good choices. Remember, you should always live on a two-way street of give and take. Will the teacher offer a high level of help because they appreciate your contributions, or not? You determine that! So, take a moment to reflect: Are you being as helpful as you can be consistently? If everyone were acting like you, what would it look like?

Chapter 26: Are You Making Your Family Proud?

Families are the compass that guides us. They are the inspiration to reach great heights, and our comfort when we occasionally falter.

— Brad Henry

Live each day as if your family were watching, ensuring every action is a proud reflection of who you are and the name you carry. Your actions, your behavior, and your choices directly influence your family's pride in you. Make them proud of you in whatever you do. Let the thought of making your family proud be a driving force in your actions, motivating you to do your best. When I was a teacher, I tried to call home to two students a week to share with their families how outstanding the students were and how much I enjoyed teaching them. That phone call was an honor, marked by daily choices that went above and beyond the call of duty. The students made great choices, choices that carry weight and significance, and made a difference in class and the school. It was always a special moment to call home, and it was always a win-win. Put yourself in the best position. There may be a moment when you receive a surprise call or have a great dialogue about you at an open house or a curriculum night. There is no guarantee that it will happen, but you need to be in a favorable position to make it possible. How will you feel if or when that happens?

Your One-Degree Shift

- Do one helpful thing around the house this week without being asked.

- Ask a caregiver or guardian about their day, and actively listen for two minutes without interrupting.

Chapter 27: Earning Trust

Trust is the glue of life. It's the most essential ingredient in effective communication. It's the foundational principle that holds all relationships.

— Stephen Covey

Some students get a lot of freedom from an adult or adults in the school. Students who are trusted have developed a reputation for consistently producing excellent and responsible work, as well as demonstrating admirable behavior. Trust takes a long time to build between people and can be destroyed in a matter of minutes. Getting involved in your school is a great way to start building trust and credibility. The longer you wait to get involved, the more likely other students will be building trust before you arrive, thus minimizing your opportunities. You must be willing to try, be helpful, work hard, and step up in your classroom to foster an increase in trust. The trust you work to build will take time and discipline from you, as you need to be consistent daily. One way to accelerate the trust is to show up early, stay late, and ask how you can help routinely. Doing so reflects a spirit of involvement and commitment that will increase adults' trust in you. When you get your chance to step out and be trusted, stay focused and nail it. Trust has to be built, and you need to get started and watch it grow. These moments of reliance are leadership in action. Building trust comes from taking action; it won't be handed to you, but you can start by being helpful each day.

Chapter 28: Are Your Actions Taxing Your Relationships with Teachers?

I've learned that people will forget what you said, people will forget what you did, but people will never forget how you made them feel.

— Maya Angelou

Do we ever consider the cost of our behaviors? Most of the time, the answer is probably no, but occasionally it is yes. This will be different for each student. For example, when a teacher teaches a class, in some cases, gum is not permitted for whatever reason. It can be an honest mistake if it happens rarely that you accidentally have gum. But if you're consistently chewing gum in that class and having to spit it out, what is that costing you? It's only gum, right? It's only gum, so why is it even an issue? The question is, what does this say about you? Indeed, it does not make you a bad person, but a teacher could think you're irresponsible, you're immature, or that you don't respect them or the class rules. That is a lot to trade for gum. It seems small, but that is what most things are made up of, small things or small choices.

It could be the same for showing up continually unprepared for class. This will not help your performance in the class and your relationship with the teacher. The teacher may see you as not caring, and you're demonstrating passive disrespect toward the class. How would you feel if you had asked multiple times for something not to happen, like gum, and a student still does it and makes excuses for its continuation? That may seem like a small thing, but it adds up to your level of cooperation and respect.

Continually failing to honor a request erodes trust. Passive disrespect is unnecessary; strive to show the highest level of respect toward all the people you come into contact with and follow their expectations.

Chapter 29: Your Daily Deposit of Respect

Show respect even to people who don't deserve it; not as a reflection of their character, but as a reflection of yours.

— Dave Willis

How challenging is it to say the words "please" and "thank you"? It's not that difficult; I'm sure you would agree. These are basic habits that can make a big difference. When you enter a class, walk by the teacher's desk if they're sitting there and make it a habit to say something small and kind, like "Good morning" or "Hello—how is your morning going?" That small gesture matters. It would matter to you also if a teacher did that in return. On the way out of class, you could walk by again and say, "Thank you."

These goodwill gestures are not just about supporting and connecting with others, including your teachers, but also about creating a culture of reciprocity. It's an offer of appreciation and gratitude. You do this not because you like them, although that helps, and you don't do it because you dislike them. That is not a standard of gratitude. You are above the line of average.

Chapter 30: Are You Ready to Go Beyond Courtesy?

Life is not so short but that there is always time for courtesy.

— Ralph Waldo Emerson

Most high school students have a basic understanding of courtesy. It's the polite, expected "thank you" when someone holds the door or helps you with a task. Gratitude, however, is a more profound emotion. It is often called the "most exquisite form of courtesy" because it adds a layer of genuine feeling to a polite act.

Think of it this way: courtesy is a handshake, a respectful and appropriate social gesture. Gratitude is a hug; it's warmer, more personal, and communicates a deeper connection. While an act of courtesy is often situational and happens in the moment, gratitude is a lasting appreciation that you can express at any time, connecting your thanks to the specific impact a person had on you.

Let's look at how this distinction plays out in real life.

- Someone helps you with your homework. When they are finished, you say, "Thank you." That is courtesy. Later that week, you stop them in the hall and say, "I just wanted to let you know how much your help with that assignment meant to me. I was really struggling, and you made it click." That is gratitude.

- A nurse brings a patient their medicine on time and checks their vitals. The patient says, "Thank you for your help." That is courtesy. Later, the patient tells the nurse, "Beyond all the medical help, I want to thank you for taking a few minutes to listen to me when I was scared. Your kindness made a difficult day so much better." That is gratitude.

In both scenarios, the courteous act was good and expected. The grateful act, however, elevated the interaction by acknowledging the personal impact, which fosters a much stronger human connection.

While it's important to continue demonstrating courtesy in your daily life, challenge yourself to take the next step. Expressing gratitude is not just about making someone's day brighter; it's a powerful tool for personal growth and development. When you make the effort to show genuine appreciation, you deepen your connections, foster empathy, and become more aware of the good around you. It's a win-win: the other person feels truly seen and valued, and you feel good about the positive impact you're making.

Chapter 31: See the Person Who Feels Invisible

If you want to lift yourself up, lift up someone else.

— Booker T. Washington

It takes a lot of courage not to be like everyone else. Our need to belong is one of the most fundamental needs we have, and social conformity and embracing group norms are often necessary to feel a sense of acceptance and inclusion. But sometimes, stepping out of the crowd can make a significant difference to someone else. To be helpful is to brighten someone's day, and it might be someone you don't know.

A simple way to step up and both develop and show your courage is to help substitute teachers on days when your regular teacher is not in your classroom. It would start by going up to a substitute teacher when you enter the class, introducing yourself, and asking if there's anything you can help them with. Then, share if they need any help, please let you know, and you will be glad to step up. It is easy to conclude that students' cooperation levels often drop on these days when a substitute teacher is in the class. This reflects a great deal about a student's character and is a sign of their high standards in lending a hand in times of need.

Think about how you treat people who don't have authority over you or don't affect your life directly. Many students excel at working with people who don't have authority over them. Unfortunately, some students treat people who lack authority over them quite poorly, including substitute teachers, lunch support staff, and bus drivers. They feel they can act this way because it will have little to no consequence. You won't have to do superhuman things, but being a supportive person is a powerful and great way to start making their day better.

Students rarely think about doing something like this, and that is precisely why you should do it. You see things others don't, which is beneficial for another person and your school. That is maturity and character in action. Be sure to say "thank you" on the way out. Remember, you have the power to create a positive school environment through your daily actions, especially in times of need, such as when you have a substitute teacher.

The final part of this section is being willing to introduce yourself to a new student and offer to help them out. This is a relatively simple idea. If you notice someone new in a class, you could stop by their desk or catch them in the hallway and simply say hello and introduce yourself. You could then ask them if they need help with anything or have any questions. Most likely, the answer would be "no," but the fact that you offered it is essential. If you were new, would you not appreciate the same? The answer is yes, so be that person. Looking outside of yourself daily, you will notice that people need help. Just be prepared to step up, and the reward will be an incredible feeling of knowing you've helped someone have a better day because of what you did.

Your One-Degree Shift

- Make a point to say hello by name to one person at school whom you normally don't talk to.

- Hold the door for someone and make eye contact with a genuine smile.

Chapter 32: Where Do You Go Above and Beyond?

The only way to discover the limits of the possible is to go beyond them to the impossible.

— Arthur C. Clarke

What is the way you go above and beyond? That's an interesting question. Teachers see anywhere from 100 to 200 students a day. If you act like everybody else, you will be just like everybody else. Going above and beyond means doing more than what is expected by taking initiative, being proactive, and showing a willingness to help others. For instance, you could offer to help a teacher with a task, assist a classmate who is struggling, or participate in extracurricular activities. This mindset of going above and beyond is not just about meeting expectations, but about exceeding them and pushing yourself to do more. It's about being proactive and taking the initiative to make a positive difference in your school community. This is the kind of attitude that will set you apart and inspire others to do the same.

Based on experience, the teaching load has increased dramatically over the past decade. Teachers are now asked to do more than ever in their careers. How can you go above and beyond? How about asking a teacher if they need any help? Most of the time, they will say no. However, the difference is that you took the time to think outside yourself, and a teacher will remember that you asked. This might change the way a teacher sees you and improve, or even start, a very positive connection that leads to a better class environment. It's free to ask, and what's the worst that happens? You give up some time to help someone else. That's a win, and it's a way you can go above and beyond.

Here are some specific examples of going above and beyond in the classroom: helping with a bulletin board, cleaning up after class, assisting with the organization of an upcoming project, filing papers, organizing the classroom, and other tasks you may think of or observe that need attention. Remember, these are just examples. Going above and beyond can be anything that helps your class and school community. Be known for being that kind of person. Everyone benefits when you choose to go above and beyond. It does not have to take a lot of time.

Chapter 33: What Does School Pride Look and Sound Like?

It's not about the bricks and mortar. It's about the spirit of the people who walk these halls, past and present.

— Unknown

You are either part of the momentum of having school pride, or you're not. What can I do, you ask? It's as simple as wearing school colors, participating in spirit weeks, decorating lockers to recognize accomplishments and participation, and getting involved in clubs, sports, band, and other activities. Attend school events, such as plays, concerts, sporting events, and art shows. Your attendance is a boost to the people who invest their time in sharing and presenting their experience with you. A united school is one that students are excited to attend. Energy is contagious, and it only takes a few people to start it. Get some friends to start moving it forward and help it grow, improve pride and spirit for everyone.

Chapter 34: Energy Is the Separator

Your energy introduces you before you even speak.

— Unknown

Doctors possess a high degree of intelligence. Having visited many doctors throughout my life for various needs has led me to consider what distinguishes doctors into excellent, good, and not-so-good categories of job performance. They have all fundamentally followed the same path to becoming a certified doctor. They have all met the same standards required for the classes taken, the exams passed, and their residency to become a doctor; so why are some so good and some not so good? What separates a good doctor from another doctor at their job? What sets a food server at a restaurant apart from the other food servers, who all take the same orders, serve food, and aim to make your visit enjoyable? These are two very different jobs with distinct skill sets in one regard, but in another way, they are very similar. What do both jobs have in common that makes a person excellent, good, or not so good in their field? I have given this question considerable thought, and I challenge you to both understand and make a difference in your daily interactions. It comes down to positive energy and genuine care for the patient. When you're in the doctor's office and the doctor finally comes in, you can feel their energy or lack of energy in how they enter and greet you. This gives you a feeling of care and regard, and is a welcome mindset toward the doctor. Or, you can tell they are not present and are just trying to treat your issue and move on with their day.

The way they listen to you and their level of attentiveness make the difference. This sincere level of care, this personal touch, is what makes you feel valued and important and makes them a good doctor. Doctors are intelligent professionals, so in most cases, they can help you get back on a healthy track. However, it is their interaction with you that determines how you feel about them. Think about that. The first few minutes of interacting with them decide whether or not you like or dislike them. The fantastic thing is that doctors often have to provide this personal care for 30 years. Imagine having to walk into a room and be 'on' and caring every time, without letting your degree of individual attentiveness slip. That is a real commitment to the people you encounter each day. They have a genuine passion to help people, and it shows.

How about being a food server? After five years of doing the same job, you still need to bring the same positive attitude and energy to each table. To be that way consistently is a mindset that others can emulate. You cannot just wake up one day and be energetic and caring toward others. It will not happen magically overnight. You need to practice this mindset so that it becomes ingrained in you and becomes a part of who you are. It does not matter what professional field you enter; energy and care will always be essential and can set people apart.

People can feel your vibe, so practice being energetic and caring each day.

People can feel your vibe, so practice being energetic and caring each day. I am sure you agree with me on that, but do you bring energy and care to school each day, or are you too tired or busy for that now?

You might also justify that you agree with what I am saying, but that doesn't apply to you yet, so it's a good idea to practice these things later. What if the doctor or food server thought that, and it was your visit? They would do it later, because they didn't feel like being energetic or caring at that moment, or that day, or that week. Work on making this mindset a part of who you are every day. Reflect for a minute at the end of each day about how you did today. This self-reflection is crucial in understanding your actions and improving your mindset. Focus on these qualities because care and energy are contagious, and people enjoy being around individuals who possess those qualities. Work to become one.

Your One-Degree Shift

- The next time you walk into a classroom or store, make a conscious effort to smile and greet the first person you see.

- When you're feeling tired tomorrow, stand up, stretch, and take 10 deep breaths instead of reaching for your phone.

Chapter 35: Be a Great Listener

Listening is a magnetic and strange thing, a creative force. The friends who listen to us are the ones we move toward. When we are listened to, it creates us, makes us unfold and expand.

— Karl A. Menninger

When people are talking to you, you may sometimes drift off and give them less respect than they deserve, but you do it unintentionally. I am always working on becoming a better listener and finding small ways to show people I care about what they have to say and that they are important. It conveys to the other person that they are essential and that you care about them. It's an easy way to make a good impression, but on the other hand, it's often a quick way to make a very poor one. I always remind my basketball team that they need to be great listeners and bring energy to practice each day. That is how much I value listening skills. And like everyone else, I sometimes don't always give my best. Every day, I take time to reflect on my day while driving home, and how I treated each person during the interactions that occurred throughout the day. This reflection is an integral part of improving your listening skills, allowing you to hold yourself accountable. By doing this, I know that next time I talk with them, I need to be more attentive and bring my "A" game. When you listen to a person, you're not just hearing them; you need to focus on understanding what they are saying or trying to say. There is a big difference in what I just shared. To focus on understanding, you're working on being present and not just hearing the words spoken.

Great listening is about understanding emotions, not just hearing words.

To be a great listener, you need a few basic skills. These include maintaining eye contact, nodding in agreement, asking follow-up questions, and showing empathy. Empathy is a vital part of listening. It's about understanding the person's perspective and emotions, not just their words. By practicing empathy, you can connect more deeply with the speaker and gain a better understanding of their feelings and thoughts. This can significantly enhance your communication and relationship-building abilities.

There are a few things you want to avoid when trying to be an active listener. One is not having your cell phone on the table or in your hand. It makes you seem less present. You also don't want to start talking before they finish sharing. I see this a lot. People will have their sentence on the tip of their tongue, ready to blurt it before the first person has even stopped talking. This tells me they stopped listening and have already started preparing a response while the first person continues to explain their point of view. When a person stops talking, pause for a second or two and reflect on what they just said. It makes you look and feel invested in correctly understanding them.

Excellent listening skills will help you make stronger connections.

Your One-Degree Shift

- In your next conversation with a friend, ask a follow-up question instead of immediately sharing your own story.

- Put your phone completely away (out of sight) the next time someone is talking to you.

Chapter 36: Read the Room

The most important thing in communication is hearing what isn't said.

— Peter Drucker

Something to note at school is the importance of group dynamics. Group dynamics change as the group's size increases or decreases. The smaller the group, the more personal and less formal it tends to be. As the group grows larger, it becomes more formal and less personal. Why does this happen? Because we perceive large groups as being less engaging and more anonymous, whereas smaller groups are perceived as more engaging and less anonymous.

Why is this important? Students often fail to read the room effectively when transitioning into larger group settings. They lack the recognition and cooperation needed for the speaker or the person in charge of leading or managing the larger group. Why do students do this? People often feel less vulnerable when in a large group. The group dynamics we perceive make us feel less at risk of consequences due to the enormity of the group. It can cause people to do things they usually would not do in a small group situation.

Why does it matter? It is a matter of courtesy and respect. Someday, you will be in charge of a larger group. It comes back to knowing how to be helpful. In these moments, being quiet and facing forward might seem obvious, but some students miss it. As the group grows, you need to be in a situation where you can self-monitor. Although it may not be spoken, it's appreciated that you recognize and do your best to make the gathering a success for everyone involved, regardless of the group size.

Chapter 37: Body Language

*What you do speaks so loudly
that I cannot hear what you say.*

— Ralph Waldo Emerson

We all communicate a great deal about how we are feeling and doing without ever speaking a word. This is always evident in sports, where one team is winning and displays positive body language, while the other team is losing and exhibits negative body language. As a coach, I address body language with my teams. I address

it mainly when it's good and occasionally when it needs improvement. We are all familiar with what good body language looks like by this point in our lives. I want you to be aware of how you carry yourself and how you come across in classes, the hallway, the lunchroom, and everywhere else in the school. As you mature, it is essential to be aware of your body language at all times. Your body language communicates your feelings and plays a fundamental role in building trust and respect among your peers. Focus on positive vibes for others to both see and pick up on. People are watching your body language as you're watching theirs. Send a good message and make yourself open and receptive to others. It makes you look more approachable and friendly, and that matters in building relationships and teamwork.

Chapter 38: When You Speak

The difference between the almost right word and the right word is really a large matter—'tis the difference between the lightning bug and the lightning.

— Mark Twain

One aspect you should consider on your path is how you speak and the words you use. Word usage is a habit. I am not judging your words; I'm challenging you to practice speaking more effectively to level up your communication skills. Filler words are a focus that many people use to fill dead air space. Often, when people are talking and come to a pause in their monologue, they will insert words while their brain is organizing its next thought. Let there be dead air space. Words like "um, um, um" are never necessary. Control your speaking pace and breathing, and slow down when speaking. It will give you more control and make you sound more confident, unlike a person searching to fill in dead air space. Remember, practicing slow and deliberate speech is a sign of respect for your audience's understanding and patience.

Words like "like," "um," "bro," "totally," and "okay" are often dead-space fillers. Focus on losing them when talking. It will take some time to develop into a habit, but you can do it if you're aware of the effort required. Often, people use these words when they get excited while talking to a group, giving a presentation, or in an interview. Practice now so you can remove the habit. Other expressions I would encourage you to lose are "do you know what I mean" and "I'm just saying." It is up to the listener to ask a question if they don't know what you mean.

The last advice I would give is to avoid using the word "hate." I hear people say they hate something, and that something is like a fancy coffee drink with too much ice, or they had a pop quiz in class today. The word "hate" is extreme, and its use should be limited to truly detestable things. Things like cancer, world hunger, and wars are hateful. When people use hate for everything, it does not make them deep because they cannot differentiate their words well. Focus on being an effective and articulate speaker, and aim to minimize the words and expressions I have covered. Remember, your word choice has a significant impact on your audience, so be responsible and considerate in your communication. Take the time to continually improve your speech, and you won't regret it.

Chapter 39: Do Not Try It Alone

If you want to go fast, go alone.
If you want to go far, go together.

— African Proverb

From your very first experiences with adults to where you stand today, you've met a wide range of grown-ups. Some brought joy and inspiration, while others may have been challenging to deal with. It's important to understand that the parents, caregivers, teachers, and coaches in your life are all committed to helping you reach heights and dreams you cannot achieve by yourself. You are currently on a path of self-discovery, still uncovering your path and purpose. Let those around you help you.

As you develop your interpersonal skills, expand your knowledge, gain wisdom, and enhance your physical and spiritual well-being. Recognize that countless people have poured their time and effort into you because they genuinely care. While some may express their support more clearly than others, each person has played an essential role in shaping who you are today and in this present moment. These present moments are aiding in your future trajectory, so demand the best of yourself.

They aren't merely clearing the path for you; they are equipping you for the journey ahead.

Stay engaged with those adults who have your best interests at heart. They matter, and they aren't merely clearing the path for you; they are equipping you for the challenges ahead, no matter what the road looks like. There is no guarantee that your path will be smooth or precisely what you dreamed it would be. The experiences they impart will prepare you for all that lies ahead. Whether the road is bumpy or soft, they prepare you to handle it. Break it down and do your best in each hour of each day, and it will start to stack up for you. Remember, you're not on this journey alone; the adults have been where you're going, so walk with them, and they will guide you. Since they are older than you, think of it this way: they walked a path and came back to get you and help you walk yours. That is an excellent viewpoint of people caring for you. Many care deeply about you and are walking alongside you, eager to offer guidance and support at every turn. Embrace their presence and wisdom, and step forward with confidence. Stay connected to those who genuinely care about you and are invested in your growth.

Chapter 40: Unlock Your Teacher's Wisdom

If I have seen further, it is by standing on the shoulders of giants.

— Isaac Newton

If a teacher has some experience under their belt, they would have had many conversations with students throughout their career. Why do I bring this up? Understand that there is only one of you, and every day is a new day for you, and a slightly new one for the teacher. They have been in days similar to this regarding their teaching instruction, sharing with the class, connecting with students, and other aspects of their work.

When teachers talk, they are sharing things in a way that benefits you. They have had their teaching and student conversations hundreds of times, helping people just like you. This makes them a valuable resource to you. You are looking at experience in motion, and you should utilize who they are and what they bring to class each day to benefit you beyond just learning the subject. Stay after class and ask them a question like, "Can I get your opinion on this regarding my college plans?" or

"Do you have good ideas on how to be better organized for the ACT or SAT?"

When you help others get what they want, you will more than likely get what you want. This is an excellent example of how being a good student can foster a positive relationship with a teacher, who will go far beyond to help you if you reciprocate by being respectful, attentive, and engaged in the learning process. If you ask a question after class and the teacher is not helpful, just move on. You only need to find one invaluable teacher to support you, and you never know who that might be. So, take a different perspective and look at a teacher as more than just someone who teaches a subject; allow them to help you figure out your life direction by gathering their input on something you need help with. You have nothing to lose and a lot to gain.

Section D: Preparing for the Path Ahead

Building strong character and positive relationships prepares you for the present moment. This final section on the mindset is about preparing for the future. Life will inevitably present you with challenges, difficult choices, and unexpected turns. The following chapters provide the tools for navigating that path ahead—from taking ownership of your mistakes to recognizing the pivotal moments that will define your journey. This is where we learn to use our mindset not just to react, but to shape our future proactively.

Chapter 41: What's Holding You Back?

If you run into a wall, don't turn around and give up. Figure out how to climb it, go through it, or work around it.

— Michael Jordan

Take a self-inventory and identify which of the dozen enemies of your success you're currently fighting against or letting win. Whichever one it is, focus on small wins in that area each day. Self-reflection is a powerful tool that allows you to identify areas for growth in the face of these challenges. Winning is not a pass/fail proposition; it's about having a growth mindset that recognizes small wins over time will add up to big wins. Keep in mind that you're not alone, and everyone battles one or more issues each day. Be demanding of yourself, but also show some grace; you deserve it. Why do you deserve grace? Because you are trying, and that is where the best version of you has to start.

Know Your Enemies: The 12 Habits That Keep You Average

Be on the lookout for these 12 enemies of your success. Identify which ones you're battling and focus on winning small victories against them every day.

- **Distraction:** Letting unimportant things, like your phone, steal your focus from what truly matters, like your goals.
- **Laziness:** Choosing what is easy and comfortable over the effort required for growth and progress.
- **Negative self-talk:** The voice in your head that tells you you're not good enough or smart enough. It's listening to your doubts instead of your potential.
- **Lack of discipline:** Doing what you *feel* like doing at the moment instead of what you *know* you should do to succeed.
- **Blaming others:** Pointing the finger at someone else for a problem you helped create, instead of taking responsibility.
- **Procrastination:** The habit of putting off important tasks until the last minute, trading future stress for present comfort.
- **Fear of failure:** Being so afraid of messing up or looking bad that you avoid trying in

the first place, which guarantees you won't succeed.

- **Perfectionism:** The trap of believing that if you can't do something perfectly, it's not worth doing at all. It's often an excuse not to start.
- **Ignoring feedback:** Closing yourself off to advice from people who are trying to help you improve, as you think you already know everything.
- **Resistant to change:** Wanting things to stay the same because it's familiar, even if a change would lead to a better outcome.
- **Lack of consistency:** Working hard one day and then doing nothing for the next three. It's starting strong but failing to follow through.
- **Comparison:** Measuring your success or happiness against someone else's life (especially their social media), which is the fastest way to feel like you're not good enough.

Chapter 42: Own Your Mistakes, Own Your Power

The moment we start to point a finger, the moment we start to blame somebody else, is the moment we give up our power.

— Barack Obama

When I was about to have a challenging discussion with a student who significantly disrupted the class, I would always tell them to

start by acknowledging what they had done and what they were responsible for. If a student takes responsibility from the start, the conversation moves along much more quickly. I would remind them that they are giving away their power in class, and I'd have to start making their seating choices, partner choices, and other choices that students usually like to be in control of. I would also appreciate the opportunity to learn and understand how I could better assist them in improving their performance in the future. It should be a straightforward dialogue and only take a few minutes.

When you refuse to take responsibility, you are giving away your power.

If a student starts with anything other than the word "I," I could see the lack of responsibility in the rest of the sentence they were about to share. Most often, it was either "I wasn't the only one" or "they told me to." These words implied that there was little to no self-responsibility, especially when in a large group; they were still responsible for their actions, as are you and I. When you're young, this sometimes seems unfair and is hard to understand. However, it's essential to avoid making excuses and take full responsibility for your actions. A defense cannot be that I wasn't the only one who did it. That might be very true and quite frustrating, but you got caught. If they were part of it and happened to get caught or cause an issue, they might have consequences. Be 100 percent responsible for yourself, and leave the poor excuses out of a challenging dialogue. Just step up and own it.

Chapter 43: Owning Your Narrative

When we deny our stories, they define us. When we own our stories, we get to write a brave new ending.

— Brené Brown

Human nature is intriguing and dependable. It's common for people to portray themselves as victims when telling their stories, especially in the context of a conflict. When events affect adults, they typically communicate these occurrences to others using vague terms like "they," the administration, or the government, which allows them to frame their experience of victimization without direct accountability or specifying who is actually responsible. But what if we change this narrative? What if we start acknowledging our shared responsibility in social interactions? This shift in perspective can make us feel more connected and part of a larger narrative.

Why do we victimize ourselves? It makes others sympathize with us, and that makes us feel better, as if we are not alone and are now understood. Well, the same thing happens in schools. Students will share a story with their peers or parents about a situation that may have seemed unfair to them. They were unfairly treated. What is often overlooked is the gradual buildup of conflict that occurs daily or weekly, which can lead to a classroom issue or even an administered consequence that now seems unfair from the victim's perspective. If a student only tells about the one moment and none of the background conflict or lead-up that they caused, it seems reasonable to see themselves as the victim. It's wise to ask what triggered the teacher's reaction and whether there have been any similar issues in the past. Work to get the whole story, not just the one critical moment, which seems unfair without proper context or background information.

Injustices or unfair moments do happen, for sure. People seldom offer up when they are rude, disrespectful, uncooperative, or exhibit some other behavior that hurts another person. Who arrives at their lunch table and says, "Boy, was I a jerk to Mr. Smith." So, when we hear these stories, we must remember that we are sometimes both the cause and the recipient of another person's poor choices. When someone claims unfair treatment, ask them what they may have contributed to the situation. To close, is it true that students work hard to avoid disruptions with consistently excellent character on display? Thank you for your contribution to the classroom and the school.

Chapter 44: All the Answers, but Where Are the Solutions?

We cannot solve our problems with the same thinking we used when we created them.

— Albert Einstein

It's interesting to observe students who consistently cause issues; they have almost memorized all the correct responses to use when speaking with a teacher or counselor about the incident, and telling them exactly what they want to hear to make the problem seem like it's understood and all is well again. Yet it happens again, or similarly, in the not-too-distant future. Why is that?

So, here's the real talk I have with those students: "Great, you've got all the answers, but do you have any solutions up your sleeve?" Having the correct vocabulary is beneficial, but what sets you ahead is turning those words into actions that resolve the issue, preventing it from being constantly repeated. It's not just about knowing what to say in a conversation; it's about taking the initiative to carry it out—words become empty if they're not put into action.

Let's be honest: Whenever a student keeps tossing around perfect answers without any solid solutions, they're handing over their power. Meanwhile, the adults then take over and start implementing changes to "support" the student. But then, guess what? The student often grumbles about the new rules or arrangements.

The takeaway? It's not just about having those correct answers—what counts are the solutions that come with them. It's a two-step dance of maturity and ownership. By adopting this approach, you're not only solving problems, but you're also taking full ownership of your learning. Additionally, this approach can rebuild trust and address issues more effectively. So, the next time you're confronted with a problem, remember: Let's swap out those perfect answers for some solid solutions and keep the drama on the stage where it belongs.

Chapter 45: "My School Sucks"—How Are You Not Part of That?

The price of greatness is responsibility.

— Winston Churchill

When I hear students say something like "my team sucks" or "my school sucks," I can feel the anger, frustration, and disappointment in their words. We have all felt that way at times, but here's the problem with those statements: they give away your power. Complaining passes the blame to others and leaves you feeling helpless, when the real goal is to take action and make a positive difference.

The bottom line of responsibility is that if you think this way about something, you should take some action to address it or simply move on and refrain from complaining about it. Remember, your actions have the power to make a positive difference. Those words are easy to say because they pass the blame onto others, and we are absolved from owning any part of the equation. Feeling a certain way is easy, but taking action to make a positive difference can be the challenge.

So, when you hear someone talk like that or make those statements, politely and calmly ask them how they plan to fix it or resolve it. Do it in a nonconfrontational way, too. Also, ask them what part of the team or the school is the problem, and be ready to listen. Flip the script. Turn the conversation toward solutions and responsibility.

Chapter 46: If I'm Not Demanding Your Best, How Much Can I Help You?

The greatest gift a leader can give is high expectations.

— John C. Maxwell

If someone is pushing you to do better, it means they care deeply about you. You may not always like it, but a person who is willing to be

demanding of you and risks not being liked by you is someone truly committed to you. That is not easy, since people generally want to be liked, and pushing you is not always a comfortable act. In the moment, you may not like it, but in the future, you will understand what caring looks and feels like. It's hard not to take it personally sometimes, but remind yourself that this situation is temporary, and you can both handle it. You will appreciate it later, as you will be the beneficiary of stepping out of your comfort zone. Focus on improving and trust the person who demands your best. It may not always be fun, but you will both grow from the experience and benefit in ways you cannot yet see.

Chapter 47: The Push You Didn't Know You Needed

The people who push you are the ones who see the potential in you before you see it in yourself.

— Unknown

The Four Stages of Competence

This is a model for learning and skill development.

Level 1—Unconscious Incompetence: "You don't know that you don't know."

Level 2—Conscious Incompetence: "You know that you don't know."

Level 3—Conscious Competence: "You know why, but you have some success." Also described as "You know that you know, but you have to think about it."

Level 4—Unconscious Competence: "You don't have to think about it; it's second nature."

As you prepare to start a new grade, remember that it serves you better to be overprepared than underprepared. The benefits of being overprepared are immense—it ensures your best chance for success and instills a sense of confidence and readiness for any challenge that may come your way. This sense of preparedness will empower you to face your next academic challenge with confidence and determination.

Reflect on a time in your educational experience when you had a teacher who either overprepared or underprepared you for the next level. All of a sudden, your liking or disliking that teacher when you had them went out the window. Now you know that the teacher who overprepared you had your best interest at heart and possessed the fourth level of consciousness, meaning that they knew what you needed to be ready for at the next level. The fourth level of consciousness is that you don't have to think about it; that is the case of the teacher who prepared you and challenged you. They served you well, and now you are reaping the benefits of their wisdom. The teacher who had the first level of consciousness, who didn't know that they didn't know, is now causing you stress and worry about keeping up and doing well, as they did not provide you with assistance. You will appreciate that the teacher who prepared you and pushed you hard knew that their demands on you then would pay off in your later schooling.

The key point is that if someone is challenging you, meet their needs and trust the process. Don't complain, as that will just weaken your mindset. Your attitude toward challenges can make all the difference. Meet your challenges with a positive mindset, and you will emerge stronger, more resilient, and more confident. Your mindset is a powerful tool that you can shape to support your academic journey, so always strive to maintain a positive outlook and accept the challenges presented by your teachers.

Chapter 48: Will You Recognize Your Moment?

Carpe diem. Seize the day, boys. Make your lives extraordinary.

— John Keating (played by Robin Williams) in *Dead Poets Society* (directed by Peter Weir, 1989)

A moment or some moments will define your high school career and your life. The question is, will you be ready? Too often, people fail to recognize that they missed a moment because they didn't perceive it as such. Most people miss their moment because it isn't obvious. They develop the mindset that every day is the same, so I can be the same. It becomes a rut and a mindset that it will make no difference to be different from yesterday.

A different perspective is the difference. Every day is a chance for something special to happen that can redirect your life in a direction you could not have imagined or wished for in a significant and better way. However, you must be prepared and actively look for it. How does that happen, and what can I do to prevent it from happening? It focuses on being the best version of yourself on an hourly, daily, weekly, monthly, and yearly basis. The more often you operate at the best version of yourself, the greater the potential for something positive to move you in a new direction. This includes consistently focusing on the anchor habits and maintaining an energetic and optimistic attitude at all times. Realize you are always on the lookout for a moment that could be profound; they happen, but will you see it that way? That is the mindset you need to develop. It's not just when you feel like it. That is what average people think. When I feel like it, I will seek it.

Treat enthusiasm as a daily decision, not a random emotion.

Treat enthusiasm as a deliberate choice, not a fleeting emotion. Many people wonder why it matters. When you come in contact with others, greet them with a smile, say hello, and be a great listener by letting them talk first. Again, we are back to the fact that what is easy to do is also easy not to do. Why would I go around and act like that? It is because people are watching and looking for individuals like that, as they have an impact on others. I often observe this when I'm out by myself and act in this way, noticing what other people are doing and how they behave.

Recently, I took a flight to New Mexico. What caught my eye was a flight attendant who was passionate about her job. She was going up and down the aisle, taking drink orders and treating everyone like a special person. It was the small things she was doing that caught my eye. It was a repetitive job, and she made it look easy and enjoyable. Later in the flight, I went to the back of the plane to use the washroom, which was occupied, so I had to wait. I struck up a conversation with her, asking her how long she had been doing her job. She said six months. I then went to share with her how well she was doing and shared that I thought she was exceptional, and she makes a difference with her small choices, ensuring everyone's flight is successful and enjoyable. She was very pleased to hear those words of appreciation. After I returned to my seat, I thought to myself, how can I further help her?

I then wrote down six books that I would suggest she read to support and help her become an even better version of herself, which will allow her, if she takes action and continues to improve, to open the door to more moments that can both change her and transform her life. I don't doubt that she will be promoted very shortly, as her effort, attitude, and dedication are truly remarkable. Her promotion would be the result of who she is daily; she chooses to be that way in her job. The other flight attendant was fine, but there was a notable difference, and it was all about the mindset and habits they had, and the standards they set for themselves. The flight attendant I spoke to was different, and it showed. That's what will separate her as she separates herself daily. Her small choices are stacking up for her.

Will you make the self-commitment to cultivate these habits and be open to meeting people who will help shape your life? People are watching, and if you are consistent in your habits and build the best version of yourself hour after hour, day after day, you can't help but have moments that will impact you. You need to realize that you're always on for doing your best work, and how you feel matters, but you still get it done.

Chapter 49: How Do You Think This Will End?

Starting strong is good. Finishing strong is epic.

— Robin Sharma

When you choose to do something that is not helpful in school, ask yourself how it will ultimately benefit you. Usually, the answer looking forward in time is not good. We often get caught up in moments and can veer slightly or significantly off course. The question to ask yourself is, "If I continue this choice or behavior, how will it end?" That will usually indicate whether or not you're on the right path with your decisions. As a teacher, I would often ask a student this single question and let them think about it in a quiet moment; usually, things would improve. Does this continued behavior choice end well, or will it end poorly?

Think ahead! Be your guide for good decisions. Remember, the power to shape your future lies in the choices you make today. The person you will become after high school will be significantly influenced by the choices you make now. Imagine you're looking back at your current actions someday. Will you be proud of the choices you made? This sense of power and proactive decision-making is what will shape your future. Choose wisely, and it will end well for you.

Answering the question from this chapter—"How will this end?"—requires honest reflection. It's about examining your daily trajectory and recognizing that small choices can lead to significant change. You have the power to make these choices. Keep stacking your essential decisions and habits, and over time, the magic will happen.

But remember the most essential part of this journey: The right doors won't open for you until you're the version of yourself that's supposed to walk through them. This isn't about working hard for a month or two; it may take years of diligent internal and external work. Are you prepared for that level of commitment?

Answering that question honestly is the first step. But reflection is nothing without action. The next step, and the focus of the chapters to come, is to actively hold yourself to a higher standard than the world around you.

Chapter 50: Everything Happens Twice—Are You Prepared?

Before anything else, preparation is the key to success.

— Alexander Graham Bell

Steven Covey, in his book *The 7 Habits of Highly Effective People*, says everything happens twice. Covey states that "beginning with the end in mind" is based on the principle that all things are created twice. There's a mental or first creation, and a physical or second creation. The

Thinking   Creating

first thing is mental, which is the first "happening" or creation of the plan, goal, idea, or conversation. The second "happening" is the physical manifestation of the mental creation. This involves putting in the effort and working toward bringing the envisioned idea in your imagination into reality. Why am I sharing this concept with you? The idea of writing this book had to happen in my mind first. This book began to take shape from its inception as a thought or suggestion, and now it's moving forward into a creation. It followed Covey's idea that everything happens twice.

Why is the need to know this important? Because you can use this idea to prepare for the inevitable challenges that will come your way. I am talking about alcohol, drugs, vaping, and sexual activity. Rehearse these conversations in your head so that when the moment arrives, you are ready to respond and avoid them. Like a performer in a play, the more you practice, the better you will know your lines. When your moment comes to decline something that falls below your standards, you will be ready to stand up for yourself. You won't have to justify your words; just share them firmly and confidently. You will feel proud of your choice because you made a plan for it. You created the words in your head, then spoke them at the correct time.

Think of this mental preparation like a fire drill. Schools don't run fire drills to test your bravery in a crisis; they run them so that when the alarm sounds, you don't have to stop and think. You react automatically because you've already walked the path. The plan is pre-loaded. Relying on in-the-moment willpower to navigate a high-pressure social situation is like trying to read the emergency exit map while the room is filled with smoke. In the chaos of the moment, a pre-made plan is always more effective than spontaneous courage.

This mental creation is about more than just deciding to say "no"; it's about building a script and visualizing the scene for your future self. Picture the environment: the music, the people, the specific moment of pressure. Then, create your lines—not just what you'll say, but how you'll say it. A simple, confident, "Nah, I'm good," or "I've got a game tomorrow; can't risk it," is often all you need. The goal isn't to be confrontational; it's to be clear and concise. This isn't just a refusal; it's a statement about the person you've already decided to be.

Ultimately, preparation enables you to decide in a calm, logical moment, rather than an emotional, high-pressure one. You are choosing your path now, so you don't have to search for it later when you might feel disoriented by the desire to fit in. By rehearsing your response, you ensure that your future actions align with your present values. This is the essence of creating things twice: the person you want to be in that challenging moment is mentally created today. When the time comes, you aren't making a difficult choice; you are simply stepping into the role you've already practiced for.

Chapter 51: How Does Your Athletic Career End?

Don't cry because it's over. Smile because it happened.

— Attributed to Ludwig Jacobowski

My basketball career underwent a dramatic transformation, transitioning from a rising player in my second year of college to one who struggled to keep up. I was playing in a game against a college team in Wisconsin when I went up for a defensive rebound and landed wrong on my right ankle. I had injured my ankles before, but this was significantly different, as the level of pain exceeded anything I had ever experienced. I recall rolling around on the gym floor for a few minutes as the pain was extreme.

After about 20 minutes of regrouping and calming down, I sat on the bench with a huge ankle that I could not feel. I figured this was due to the trauma of the injury. We rode home in the bus for five hours, and I called my mom to come and pick me up. We went to emergency care in my hometown, where, after X-rays, the doctor told me I had a very severe sprain. So, I went home and iced my ankle on and off for three days, but I still couldn't feel my foot.

Again, this ankle sprain was different. On the third day, I told my mom about my numbness in my ankle, and she made an appointment with an orthopedic surgeon. We arrived at his office, and I was immediately sent into a room. He asked me some questions and then said, "I think I can save your leg."

I just lost it and started to cry, wondering what was happening and why. The doctor shared that I had compartment syndrome and he needed to operate within the hour. They started prepping my leg by shaving it in the office while we talked. I was scared as hell. I could lose the lower part of my right leg! I went immediately to surgery, and when that was over and I was well enough to be released after a day, I had to go home and elevate my right leg on two pillows for the next six weeks with no exceptions. I had to do everything with my leg elevated, including washing my hair and eating. It was a very challenging time, both physically and emotionally. I lost 30 pounds in six weeks of being in bed.

When I returned to school, a new semester had already begun, and I had to make up the finals from the previous semester. I was on crutches for another month at school. When summer arrived, I was able to start being active and began working my way back. I got back on the court, but something was not right athletically. I could feel that my right foot was not responsive; and, it turned out, it would never be again, as I lost about 50 percent of the bounce in my step. Now, I had to always land on two feet, since my right foot lacked the strength that would never return. Moving forward, I played one more year of college basketball, which was a struggle because nothing came easy anymore. I retired after my third year, and my dream of playing beyond college came to an end.

Participating in high school athletics is a privilege and the opportunity of a lifetime. The friendships, lessons, and experiences are both priceless and exceptional, offering invaluable learning opportunities. That is the essence of the high school sports experience. What people don't often consider is how it ends. The end of a sports career can be a challenging time, and it's essential to be prepared for it or at least consider the possibility. However, it is rarely discussed and often comes as a surprise. Most high school athletes make it through the first year of their chosen sport or sports by being on a team and getting some playing time. A first-year experience is usually a rewarding experience for players. After the first year of high school sports, the desire for playing time and contributing to the team in game situations takes a challenging turn for many. Please consider that your career can end with an injury, not making the team, or not playing while on the team. These are very tough endings to something we have invested a lot of time into and care about being good at, and contributing to a group of people we have likely been with for many years.

It is tough in the moment to see a dream end, but a new one can begin when you are ready.

Additionally, you may be a skilled player, but the coach wants to take the team in a different direction than your current skills allow. All these things hurt and make us feel bad. I just want to share that you are not alone. Understand that all sports careers do end, and at times, it feels like the end of the world when it happens. I've been there, feeling like my world was crumbling when my sports career came to an end. However, I persevered and found new opportunities. You can, too. When one door closes, another opens. Think about how to utilize your newfound free time to improve in another area or embark on a new path of self-discovery.

You see, from my dramatic experience of a lifelong dream ending out of my control, I got to take a new path and become a much better version of myself than the one who played basketball. It's difficult at the moment to see a dream end, but a new one can begin when you're ready.

Chapter 52: Your Path

Set your life on fire. Seek those who fan your flames.

— Rumi

Whether you know it or not, you're walking a path at this moment in your life. It is an excellent road for your personal growth and future. It may not be the exact path you desire, but view it as preparing you for something positive in your future. A challenging road early is not your destiny as you become an adult. You can rise above a difficult path, as you can always choose your response to a situation. Your path should be uplifting and make you optimistic each day. Your path choices should not compromise your character, self-respect, dignity, optimal performance, or future opportunities.

Do you ever consider changing your path? If you do, two forces are working against you. One is the need to fit in somewhere and belong to something, and the other is the thought of walking alone. When I was younger, I wouldn't have even considered doing this; and in hindsight, I wish I had both the idea and the courage to walk my path, even if it meant going it alone for a while.

Why change paths if you need to? Because there are people your age walking the path you want to be on, and if you change yours, you will meet them. If you don't feel the need to change your path, you won't meet them because they're on a path you've chosen not to follow, and you'll be going your separate ways. It's that simple. When you go for a hike, for example, the path you choose to hike matters in determining who you will meet along the way. If you don't walk on that path for your hike, you will not meet the people going that way because you will not be there. You may start alone, but if it's a good road, have faith that others you don't know yet will also choose to walk it, and you can meet them later in your life.

Many people are choosing the right path for themselves, and to walk alongside them, you must join that path quickly if you have not already done so. The longer you wait, the further behind you will be. Remember, your personal growth and future opportunities are at stake, so act quickly to join a better path if necessary. Don't be afraid to walk alone for a while; it's only temporary.

Chapter 53: What Is an Hour of Your Life Worth?

Your time is limited, so don't waste it living someone else's life.

— Steve Jobs

There's a saying that graveyards are full of people who thought they had more time. Life is fleeting, and we have limited time. It's interesting to me how people can be so conservative with their money and unwilling to part with it, yet waste so much of their life doing meaningless things that take

them nowhere and leave them unchanged. Continuous phone scrolling is an example of lost time spent. Money is something you can acquire more of, whereas time is finite and, unlike money, you never know how much you have. Time is a currency for which we will never know our balance. Why do I bring this up? Because the only time you have is right now. We feel like we are guaranteed tomorrow because of the pattern of having so many days in a row that seem the same, and where not much changes in moments of our lives. We can become too casual about our use and value of time, often procrastinating on connecting with important people and pursuing the dreams we have. This realization should create a sense of urgency to make the most of our time.

Value your time and use it to bless others.

Value your time and use it to bless others, grow in your skills and personal skills, and make our world a better place. Don't consistently waste it on binge-watching videos, scrolling for hours, or complaining that you are bored. I am all for having downtime for a recharge, but be wise about where your downtime is taking you and how much attention you give to something during that downtime moment. Time is precious, and so are you. Take the time and effort each day to be positive, develop new skills within yourself, and perform acts of kindness, gratitude, courage, honor, and grace. You will not regret spending your time on these things. Remember, developing your skills is a robust set of tools that can empower you to make a positive impact on the world.

Chapter 54: When Three Minutes Equals Sixty

A man who dares to waste one hour of time has not discovered the value of life.

— Charles Darwin

Here is a life lesson that some high schoolers need to hear and understand. The amount is not enough to justify the choice. When does

three minutes equal 60 minutes? For example, when you are late to class, it is standard practice for the teacher to issue a detention after three tardies have occurred. I always ask why you would trade three minutes of your time for 60 minutes of boring detention. Most often, a typical response to a detention warning is that "I was only 30 seconds late." Late is late.

We sometimes use the amount of our infraction to justify or rationalize our actions. To move to a more extreme, I only had *a little* alcohol, I only stole *two* dollars, and I only cheated *a little*. It's essential to understand that rules and expectations are in place for a reason, and honoring them is a sign of responsibility and respect.

Think about it for a second: Someday, you may be in charge of a group of people as a supervisor. As a supervisor, you may have a policy prohibiting the use of cell phones during work hours. What do you do when one of your employees keeps violating the policy, but their defense is that the calls are only two minutes long, so it's not a significant issue? How do you handle it? What if it keeps happening, but only for a short time? How about when an employee shows up, often a few minutes late, and has a fancy coffee from a coffeehouse? They do it only once or twice a week and miss only five minutes of work each time. Only doing it a little does not make it acceptable. Realize this when you're young, so you don't put yourself in a bad position where three minutes equals 60 minutes. As you get older, the consequences are much more drastic as an employee.

This concept reflects a choice to be late for class, and if you are, you accept the responsibility for tardiness. There are times when things happen beyond your control, such as a sudden illness, a bathroom issue, or a teacher talking to you for too long, all of which can cause you to be late. That is not the point here. Your job is to arrive at class on time consistently. When it's an issue beyond your control, your consistency and integrity will speak for you.

Chapter 55: Think About the Next Generation

The strongest principle of growth lies in human choice.

— George Eliot

Let's go back a generation or two in your lineage; you can even go back further in time if you wish. What I want you to consider is that people in your family tree have either done things or not done things that are currently allowing and benefiting your current existence and standard of living. Your parents, grandparents, even great grandparents, and beyond have endured, suffered, made hard choices, sacrificed, and more that have allowed you to be in the exact moment in time that you're currently living in. We may not know precisely what they have done, but it required grit, resilience, and determination for them to keep moving forward.

Life has become more convenient in the past 50 years, and the people in your family tree did not have it as easy as you do. You may not even feel you have it easy, but realize it was even more difficult the further back in time you go. So, let's turn the corner. You are either doing things that will support or hinder the line of people in your family tree; what you do matters. It's not just about your life, it's about the legacy you leave. You, too, will be an earlier generation someday, so strive for your best life, as it can and will impact generations to come, or even three. It matters, and you now know you have an impact on people down the road, so look ahead and pass something on.

Conclusion to Part 2: The Mindset

As we draw this chapter to a close, it's essential to take a moment for self-reflection. These chapters have highlighted the importance of recognizing our patterns and behaviors, enabling us to identify where making better choices can lead to greater fulfillment. Implementing new habits, no matter how small, can create a ripple effect that enhances our well-being and propels us toward our goals. By embracing a mindset of continuous improvement, we empower ourselves to break free from limiting tendencies and foster a life rich with purpose and intention. Each small decision we make lays the groundwork for our future and molds the character we embody.

Keep this in mind as you move forward. The ability to reflect, adapt, and evolve is a gift only we can give ourselves. With this knowledge, we can stride confidently into the next chapter, ready to cultivate the life we envision and the habits that will take us there. The pursuit of growth is not merely about reaching a destination, but about transforming ourselves along the way, which enhances both who we are and who we can become. Trust in your abilities, trust in your journey, and trust that the path you're building is the right one. This trust is the foundation for the ultimate mindset shift: learning from those who have demonstrated extraordinary resilience in the face of impossible odds.

Part 3: Mindsets in Action

Section E: The Principles of Consistent Action

In Part 2, we did the crucial work of shaping our mindset—defining our character and learning to manage our inner world. But a mindset without action is just a collection of good ideas. This is where we turn those ideas into results. Part 3 is your practical toolkit for execution. We'll begin in this first section by exploring the fundamental principles of consistent action, the engine that drives all meaningful progress.

Chapter 56: Will a Simple Daily Habit Matter?

Habits are the compound interest of self-improvement. The same way that money multiplies through compound interest, the effects of your habits multiply as you repeat them.

— James Clear

There are many intelligent people in high schools across the country. A high GPA is just one way you're representing yourself as smart and hard-working. Do you ever wonder what else you represent or how you present yourself to others?

The other ways you describe or define yourself come down to your daily choices.

These choices are not just about today; they are about your future. You should use these choices to develop the school habits that will also prepare you for your career and gainful employment. Do you ever think that far ahead? You should be. You cannot wake up one day and just turn it on.

Think of your school day as an opportunity to practice building positive habits, so when the time comes, you'll be ready for the challenges that come your way. You should be active in class discussions and work collaboratively with teachers and peers, be consistent in your homework, and do your best to follow school expectations. If you move these skills and mindsets forward eight to 10 years, you see how they would directly transfer into employment. You should be focusing on consistency in these areas.

Separate yourself from the many other intelligent people in high school by *how* you're doing the positive habits. Choose to be respectful and energetic each day, regardless of how you're feeling. You are building your daily habits to prepare for your future. They are foundational to personal success and wellness.

Chapter 57: Your Actions Are Your Loudest Voice

*You are what you do, not what you say
you'll do.*

— Attributed to Carl Jung

Words often have a high level of value in many relationships and conversations. This is because the people speaking them back up their words with a high level of action and self-accountability. I highly value the words I share with people. What I say is what I mean, and when I say I will do something, it will happen—barring some extenuating circumstances. My words represent my integrity and reliability to others. When I was younger, that was not the case. Looking back, I realize my words were cheap and had little value, especially considering the circumstances I was facing in high school. I said what people wanted to hear, but I often didn't follow through on my promises. As I have grown older, I treat my words with the value of gold and strive to live up to them, as they represent me and my character.

While I strive for perfection, I am not immune to the disappointment caused by those who talk but don't act. I find it difficult to respect those who don't follow through on their words or show care when it's needed, particularly regarding something they have said. As a teacher, I valued every student's words until they were taken for granted or they became devalued by the student's repeated actions.

How do you cheapen your words so they have little value? You often fail to follow through on your words, which can erode your credibility. We all know people like this. They can be frustrating to be around if you're trying to accomplish something. They are acceptable just to hang out with, but not worthy of doing much more than that because you lack trust in what they say, and that can cost you time, grades, money, etc. It leads to frustration and excuses if you hold them accountable. This is why your actions are the loudest thing about you; if they back up your words at a very high level, your words are gold. If they don't match often enough, your words are cheap. Do your words meet a gold standard?

Your One-Degree Shift

- The next time you tell someone you will do something ("I'll call you later" or "I'll send you that link"), set a reminder on your phone and do it.

- Think of one small promise you made to yourself and keep it today.

Chapter 58: Unlocking Your Agency

The greatest sign of success for a teacher...is to be able to say, "The children are now working as if I did not exist."

— Maria Montessori

Agency is essential because it empowers you to shape your life and handle challenges effectively. It's the difference between things happening to you and you making things happen.

Developing agency means you're no longer passively receiving information from a teacher. Instead, you take responsibility for your own learning and growth. If you don't understand something, you take the initiative to figure it out. Your teacher becomes a guide, but you're in control. This shift is essential for success both in school and beyond.

Life doesn't get easier; you just get better at handling it. Agency is the key to improvement. By developing skills such as independence and self-direction now, you're preparing for future challenges in college, your career, and personal life. You learn to rely on yourself to find solutions and navigate complex situations. When you see your choices and actions lead to real results, your confidence grows. You learn that you can influence outcomes and overcome obstacles. This builds resilience, making it easier to bounce back from setbacks because you know you have the power to change your circumstances. In short, agency puts you in charge of becoming the person you want to be.

Agency puts you in charge of becoming the person you want to be.

Chapter 59: How Do You Use Your Power?

*When I dare to be powerful—to use my
strength in the service of my vision—then
it becomes less and less important
whether I am afraid.*

— Audre Lorde

Every person has personal power. Some people feel and show it all the time, while others feel and show it sometimes, and still others never feel it or show it. You need to be seeking growth in your power. As a young person, you increase your power when you think and do the right things, take charge of your learning as you develop your agency, and make choices that help you grow and challenge you. You feel more confident and connected when you're increasing your power. It's evident in your body language, the topics of conversation, the people you attract to form your social group, your engagement in class, and how often you smile and seem energetic. All of these, and more, contribute to your path toward greatness, as described in Chapter 3.

When you attend a class, focus on the content, engage in discussions, and prepare well for tests and quizzes, you feel more empowered, which increases your confidence and sense of self-leadership. Even when you seek extra help and stay up to date with the class's learning and content, as opposed to falling behind, not understanding what's happening in class, and letting the information pile up, it becomes overwhelming. It lessens your power and the way you interact with the world because you're giving your power away, and as a result, you feel less powerful. Observe people in your school or classes and note who appears to feel powerful or powerless. Ask yourself why you think they feel that way, and how they are showing it.

On the other hand, if you attend class without paying attention, are inactive, spend time on your phone discreetly, fail to grasp the class lesson, and take no action, you're losing or giving away your power. Your confidence will wane, and you will start to make excuses, like claiming that you're not good at this subject; or, if your grade is not good, it is because the class is too hard for you, or something else to let yourself off the hook. This mentality of weakness will allow and justify poor performance, and again, you are giving away your power.

At times, you will struggle. It's your response to the struggle that will increase your control over how you feel about your performance. It comes down to how you respond. Self-reflection is a key part of this process. It's not a predetermined, universal destiny; it's about owning your choices and actively deciding who you choose to be each day. Your power does not stand still; it's either climbing and growing stronger or it is shrinking. This is why some students feel empowered, while others struggle to get through the day with little energy, optimism, and social engagement, versus those who feel empowered and are active, involved, energetic, and optimistic. They know and feel their power. Your choices and habits will either amplify or diminish your power.

Chapter 60: Have Your Own Standards

The standard you walk past is the
standard you accept.

— David Hurley

In his book *Never Finished*, former Navy SEAL David Goggins shares a powerful story about the difference between meeting the standard and setting your own. It's a lesson that has stuck with me, and it perfectly illustrates what it means to defy average.

During the grueling Air Assault class, Goggins and his classmates were required to do a certain number of pull-ups and push-ups every time they passed under the campus entrance arches. On the very first morning, Goggins noticed another student who didn't simply meet the requirement. While everyone else dropped from the bar after their required pull-ups, this student kept going, doing far more than what was asked. He wasn't just paying the toll; he was investing himself.

Later that day, the class faced a long march with heavy packs. Goggins, a confident athlete, was in the lead pack. But as the miles wore on and the terrain got tougher, his group started to slow down and conserve energy; the logical thing to do.

But the other student didn't slow down. He was competing against his own perceived limits and operated by a different set of rules—his own.

As Goggins writes, he realized that the other student wasn't there to simply graduate. He was there to see what he was made of; to grow and push his own boundaries. The instructors didn't set his standard; it was an internal benchmark that was far higher than what anyone else expected of him. While the rest of the class was content with being above average, this student was in his own league because of his mindset (paraphrased from *Never Finished* by David Goggins).

That story perfectly illustrates what it means to have your own standards. Most people operate on a bell curve, measuring themselves against those around them. They aim to be better than average. But the people who achieve truly great things—the outliers—aren't looking at the bell curve at all. They are driven by an internal desire to find their own limits.

It takes courage and an uncommon mindset to do more than what is required, especially when no one is watching. It's about understanding that the real competition is with the person you were yesterday. Are you willing to push yourself in whatever you're pursuing, not just to pass the test or make the team, but to become an outlier? Most people are not, because it requires a level of intentional effort that goes beyond just showing up.

Start by setting your own standards today. Don't wait for a coach or a teacher to tell you what's expected. Decide for yourself what your best looks like, and then hold yourself to that, regardless of what everyone else is doing. That is the first step to moving off the crowded bell curve and onto your own path.

It takes time, commitment, dedication, grit, passion, vision, and more. Here we are back to being intentional again. Are you willing to push yourself in whatever arena you are working in or pursuing to become an outlier? Most people are not. Why? It takes a unique mindset and a level of intentional suffering to become an outlier in something. Suffering is the passionate pursuit of your dream that shapes your vision.

To wait until tomorrow is wasting today.

Having high standards is the start. Growing those standards in clarity and commitment over time as you progress is essential to keep moving the line and keep you uncomfortable, allowing you to grow. It also includes doing the work consistently, regardless of how you feel. Your determination has to be stronger than your excuses: "I'm tired," "I have a lot to do," "I don't feel like it today," or "nobody will care if I miss a day." You can always find a reason to justify a feeling. You permit yourself to fail by accepting your excuses. This is how and why people stay in a comfort zone: because they are doing just fine, or so they think.

As the sun comes up this morning in your town, remember the proverb: "The best time to plant a tree was 20 years ago. The second-best time is now." If you haven't yet created self-standards that are exceptionally high for you, then today is the day. Waiting until tomorrow is wasting today. Start with a few standards and gradually expand them. If you struggle at times, don't quit. Small steps are better than no steps at all.

Your One-Degree Shift

- Identify one area where you've been "meeting the standard" instead of setting your own. Decide on one small thing you can do to go beyond the minimum.

- The next time your friends start to complain, choose not to join in.

Chapter 61: The Tipping Point You Can't See

If it's easy to do, it's easy not to do.

— Jim Rohn

I went to pick up some food for my wife, daughter, and me at a local restaurant. When I walked in, an older teenage girl was working as the cashier and order taker. I greeted her, and she asked, "What would you like to order?" I told her my wife's order, then my daughter's order, and took a moment to consider my own before finally placing it. She read it back to me with great energy, speaking very clearly and exceptionally well.

I asked, "Excuse me, but can I be nosy for a second? Are you in high school or college?" She said she had just graduated from high school. After a moment, I asked, "What are you doing next?" She shared that she *just* wanted to become a biomedical engineer. I told her that you don't *just* become anything; you become great at whatever you choose to be, and you shouldn't minimize your aspirations.

A minute later, I said, "I bet you get all A's at school." She was surprised and asked, "How did you know?" I told her, "I can tell because you reflect it in who you are. You are a very present teenager, which is exceptional." I added, "I'm very impressed as I look for people like you who leave clues on the success path they are on. You may not realize it, but I see them in you."

She told me that it was the best thing she had heard all month, and she seemed very appreciative and emotional about it. I said, "You'll do great; I can tell." I then asked her a standard question of mine: "Do you like to read?" She replied, "Not really, but sometimes." I noted that she must have her standards to get all A's, and she confirmed that she did.

I suggested, "Why don't you read just 10 pages a day? That will add up to 300 pages a month and 12 books a year." I explained that being a reader isn't a pass/fail idea. Reading is often viewed as an all-or-nothing proposition, but if you read just 10 pages a day, it will accumulate. You might not think it would make a difference right away.

I then shared one of my favorite stories about how eating one donut won't impact your

life, but if you ate one every day for a week, you might get sick of them. I continued, "Let's take it further. If you ate a donut a day for 10 years, would it make a health difference?" She agreed that it certainly would. I said that the same principle applies to reading 10 pages a day. It might not seem significant today or tomorrow, but like the donut, there is a tipping point that you can't see yet.

Before leaving, I observed her taking an order from two elderly ladies with great kindness. I approached her, gave her a $20 bill, and left before she noticed what it was, as she quickly put it in her pocket. I mention this because it illustrates how to practice gratitude and recognize what's easy to do, which is also easy not to do.

What easy habit will you start that will benefit you in the long run? I was able to challenge her mindset, and her responsibility to put this basic, yet profound concept into action. Be patient and just get started. Even if the results may be years away, the process has begun to create a better future and a better version of you.

Your One-Degree Shift

- Pick one simple, positive habit from this book (like drinking a glass of water when you wake up) and commit to doing it tomorrow morning.

Chapter 62: Learning the Lesson Today

Life lessons will be repeated until they are learned.

— Frank Sonnenberg

How you treat people, including yourself, matters in life. Think about lessons that are often learned as a young person trying to make friends. When you were a young child, if you treated someone poorly, you learned pretty quickly that they would most likely not want to be around you or be your friend. If you treated them kindly and you were pleasant to be around, you learned that they would like you and want to be your friend.

This is a straightforward concept, yet people still struggle to grasp it as they age. As a result, they often struggle to treat others well and have difficulty forming and maintaining friendships. These are lifelong social skills that are essential to personal happiness and effective connection with others.

This is why being socialized at a young age is so important. It's not just about making friends, but about learning life lessons that are beneficial and will repeat themselves to help you grow and understand, to help you become the best version of yourself. If you don't know how to treat people, then the lesson will continue to repeat itself until you do. Most people will not hang around a negative person for an extended time.

Another typical example of a lesson that will be repeated until it is learned is the importance of self-worth and boundaries. When students start to date in high school, relationships can become very challenging. You might have your boundaries in your mind, but are you willing to stand up for yourself before the relationship becomes physical?

Young people often do things with their partner that they later regret and would not normally do because they feel the other person will not like them if they don't go along. **Think about it for a second:** If you have to do things you don't want to in a relationship to either keep your partner or get some attention, then you're compromising your self-worth.

This is an unhealthy start to learning about relationships, and it may be even harder in the next one, as you may develop a reputation that works against you. You can control your character, but you cannot control your reputation, as some people gossip and talk about others. You must know your truth, stand up for yourself, and be confident in your boundaries. If you continually find yourself in the same challenging situations, ask yourself, "Are you learning the lesson to avoid returning to the same problem?"

Chapter 63: Focus on the Process, Not the Outcome

Success isn't always about greatness. It's about consistency. Consistent hard work leads to success. Greatness will come.

— Dwayne "The Rock" Johnson

Concentrate on the process, rather than the final result. You can't dictate earning an A, but you can manage your preparation. When I coach a basketball team, I always emphasize aspects within our control rather than the

result. The outcome is uncertain, as it's yet to happen, and I can only influence the present moment. In practice, we focus on daily improvements by committing fewer errors and consistently setting higher-level challenges that lead to new opportunities for growth both as individuals and as a team. Making enough successful plays during a game will help us achieve the desired result. This principle applies to homework, quizzes, and tests. While you can't ensure an A, you have control over the amount of time you invest in preparation.

This investment will enhance your comprehension of the material to the effort you put into mastering it, enabling you to respond correctly to each question, which leads to an A. Ongoing dedication to learning the subject matter will accumulate successes in assignments, quizzes, and exams, resulting in an A by the end of the semester. Therefore, understand that while the outcome is beyond your control, you can determine your level of dedication, effort, and commitment toward achieving the results you want.

Chapter 64: Every Day Is a Tryout

The fight is won or lost far away from witnesses—behind the lines, in the gym, and out there on the road, long before I dance under those lights.

— Muhammad Ali

When do tryouts begin? The most common and straightforward answer is when the teacher or coach posts the date on a bulletin board, in a newsletter, or through some other form of communication. Most people moving toward high school have some idea already about what they might try to play or participate in, and when tryouts begin. The most insightful mindset and accurate answer is that they started a long time ago.

Have you considered tryouts as a continuum of where you're at precisely this point in your 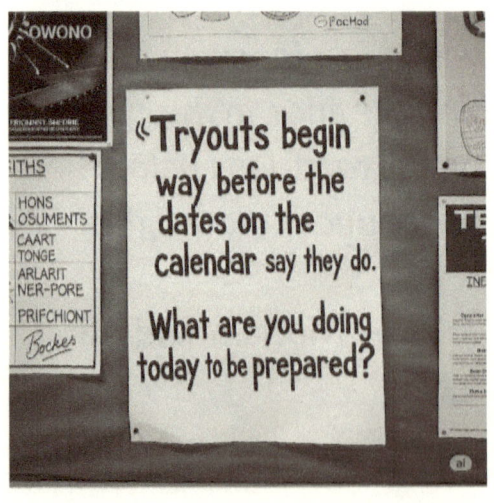 life going forward? If you're in 8th grade and want to play on the high school basketball team, when do the tryouts start? The easiest answer is the first week in November. That is a mindset that is short on vision and lacks foresight. What if you did everything a year or two years in advance to be as ready as possible, and started preparing well in advance for the actual tryout session? In your mind, you're already trying out each day, so when the moment comes, you just keep being you and doing what you have been doing all along. You don't need to step up because you have set your standards for the pursuit of your goals and dreams. Action in advance is a great way to make them happen.

Hope is a feeling, but it won't move you forward toward what's truly important to you.

I hear too many students saying, "I hope I do well." Hope is a feeling, but it won't move you forward toward what's truly important to you. If I had a flat tire on my car in my driveway and went inside my house, hoping it would get pumped up, do you think the hope I have for my tire would inflate it if it were flat? Hope will not fix the flat tire. Work has to be done on the tire. You don't go into your tryouts just hoping to do well. It takes work. You have to go into your tryouts knowing that you have prepared for a long time for this moment, and it's just another day of doing what you have been doing for years. Alternatively, you can rely on the "Hope Plan," which requires minimal daily effort and leaves you unprepared on the day of tryouts. Be prepared and act as if tryouts are very soon, so you will put in the daily work and be ready.

You are assertive and have a humble mindset that acknowledges your worth. You keep your mindset quiet and stay humble, but on the inside, you know what you have worked for.

Here is an example I have of my mindset. As I have shared, I have shot a basketball hundreds of thousands of times over my lifetime. I spent my childhood honing that skill. I just always enjoyed it and still do. When I play, I don't get excited or happy when I make a shot; I expect it to go in. Why? Because I have put in so much work and practice, I just get more focused when I miss. Shooters in basketball know that they expect to make it and focus more when they miss. They have put in the sweat to make it happen. When I watch people play, I can tell how much work they have put in, as most often when they make a basket, they smile and are so pleased. That is because they are surprised. Watch a highly skilled player; they expect it to go in and are not surprised when it does.

I'd like to share a perspective or mindset that I encountered while teaching physical education in middle school. When it was time for warm-ups, I wouldn't say much about a student's effort level in the first few weeks of school. Let them get situated and learn the routine. Then I would pose questions like, "Who plans to participate in a sport in high school?" and ask them, "When are the tryouts?" They would always give me a month or an approximate date for their sport. I would ask them, "Haven't the tryouts already started?" You can think differently and use this time to train for it every day. You have the opportunity to improve as an athlete each day you come here. Do you have the courage to work hard in front of your peers who either do not have the same vision or are too busy joining a group where working hard is not cool?

Haven't the tryouts already started?

I would tell my students who start to set their standards so they are on the right track. I would encourage them constantly. To achieve something in the future, the best way to do so is to prepare beforehand. I will repeat it: you have to be there before you get there! Consider being proactive and being prepared. You only get one chance. Don't let hope be your plan.

Section F: Strategic Action for Success

Understanding the basic principles of consistent action is like knowing how an engine works. Now, it's time to learn how to steer. The following chapters focus on strategic action—the specific choices and tactics you can use to navigate your path to success. We'll move from the "what" of doing the work to the "how" of doing it intelligently.

Chapter 65: The Extra Mile Is Never Crowded

Today I will do what others won't, so tomorrow I can accomplish what others can't.

— Jerry Rice

When I was about 11 years old, a new neighbor, Aaron, moved in behind me. I still remember the day Aaron came over to introduce himself, as we were close to the same age. Aaron and I

 quickly became friends and did many things together over the next few years. We mostly played sports with all the other neighborhood friends. As time passed, Aaron went to high school while I was in junior high school; he was three years older. We still hung out in the summer as we had done before, but we did less during the school year as we got older due to commitments to school.

Then, my first year of high school was about to start, and we would now be in high school together. I was excited, but, as you know, it would also present many academic challenges. Aaron encouraged me to join

cross-country in my first year of high school, so I signed up before school even started. He had already been a member of the cross-country team for two years. Here is where Aaron taught me a life lesson, although I didn't realize it at the time.

At 5:30 a.m. on my first day of high school, I heard Aaron knocking on my back door. I got up and went to the back door, and there was Aaron, all dressed in his running clothes—at 5:30 in the morning. I had no idea what he was doing or thinking. My first thought was, "What is he doing here?" My mindset was still built to stay comfortable at all times. He told me to get dressed so we could go for a run before school. I made my way back to my room and got dressed in whatever I could find for that morning's run. I was not prepared or organized for this run. He said we were only going to run 3 or 4 miles that day. I didn't know any better, so I agreed to go because he was older and had already been a cross-country runner for the past two years.

The morning run became a daily habit from that moment on during my first year of cross country. I remember going on those morning runs so early, and nothing felt better than having my day started that way. Aaron was an experienced varsity runner, and I was new to the team, so I listened to him. I became a running machine and never really felt exhausted from running, thanks to Aaron's vision, friendship, and dedication. At practice, we would then run 6-10 miles per day, which seemed pretty easy when I look back. I had little running experience, but my mental toughness was growing as a result of all this.

I remember my first race. I was new to the team, and the coach had given me little attention up to that point in the early part of the season. We had about 60 runners in my first race, and I just went out there, having only been running for about three weeks, and finished in 11th place. I had zero experience running and pacing in races, as it was my first year. My coach became a lot more attentive to me after that first race, and I realized I was making progress with the extra morning work I was doing.

Unfortunately, I hurt my knee a few weeks later, and that ended my first season. My takeaway, which I did not realize at the time, is that if you do things like everyone else, you will be just like everyone else. Aaron helped by showing me how not to do everything like everyone else, and I saw the difference in my early-season results.

If you do things like everyone else, you will be just like everyone else.

I wish that lesson had stuck with me in my high school years. It was only years later that I realized this and implemented it daily. As I occasionally see on a T-shirt, *hard work is undefeated*. Extra time adds up and moves you forward, as it did for me in that moment of my life, but I did not make the connection until years later. If you plan to be different from the crowd, you have to do things differently. What will you prioritize in your current situation and for your future, dedicating extra time to it?

Your One-Degree Shift

- Stay five extra minutes after practice, class, or your study session to review one thing you learned.

- When a teacher gives you an optional assignment or extra credit, do it.

Chapter 66: Seize the Moment, Choose Your Words, Value Your Time

How we spend our days is, of course, how we spend our lives.

— Annie Dillard

Being energetic, being optimistic, and doing small acts to deepen your greatness is a great mindset to approach each day as if it were a

lifetime. Get through each moment, moment by moment. It's that pursuit and mindset that will be noticed and contagious, aiding your life. If you choose to be this way and pursue the work to create this habit, you will have much less regret with three things you can never get back. Those things are some of your most valuable resources: time, words, and opportunity. So often, people misuse them and either don't even realize it or regret not being ready for their moment.

The focus is that you're always prepared because you value your time and have established standards that prevent you from being unprepared for opportunities, thanks to a growth mindset. Being prepared gives you a sense of control and empowerment, ensuring that you're always ready to seize the right opportunities. This contagious pursuit and mindset will inspire and motivate others around you. Be kind with your words, use your time wisely, and seize your opportunities as they arise. Keep in mind that sometimes opportunities don't reveal themselves, and you have to create them by stepping up and being ready.

Chapter 67: Circles of Value

Be courteous to all, but intimate with few;
and let those few be well tried before you
give them your confidence.

— George Washington

Do you ever stop and think about how we receive feedback or how we value other people's input? I am referring to how people tend to assign the same input value to everything they hear, regardless of the source.
When we operate in this manner, we often listen to what we want to hear and don't filter the source.

strangers
people we know
friends
best friends
family
you

I would like you to begin filtering your sources. Not all levels should have the same value to you. I want to point out to you and have you critically examine those who have your best interests at heart.

Your first and tightest circle around you as a person is your immediate family. They will speak from the heart to share things with you with positive intent. Then you have your inner circle of best friends. Be careful and guard this inner circle of friendships. They should be supportive and demonstrate these qualities: loyalty, honesty, unconditional support, and being there when things get tough. Just because you hang out with someone does not put them in your inner circle. They may be just part of your social group. People often talk too much and reveal too much to everyone because they fail to filter their social circle appropriately.

The remaining groups are evident in terms of how you deal with the circles. I see too many people taking feedback from the outer circles and making their words more important than those of the two inner circles. Especially when the feedback is negative, remind yourself that you assign value to the input you receive, so don't overvalue a stranger's feedback. Filter your input and guard your innermost circles.

Read the following words from President Theodore Roosevelt:

It is not the critic who counts; not the man who points out how the strong man stumbles, or where the doer of deeds could have done them better. The credit belongs to the man who is actually in the arena, whose face is marred by dust and sweat and blood; who strives valiantly; who errs, who comes short again and again, because there is no  effort without error and shortcoming; but who does actually strive to do the deeds; who knows great enthusiasms, the great devotions; who spends himself in a worthy cause; who at the best knows in the end the triumph of high achievement, and who at the worst, if he fails, at least fails while daring greatly, so that his place shall never be with those cold and timid souls who neither know victory nor defeat.

— Theodore Roosevelt

Chapter 68: Your Inner Compass: The Art of Making the Right Call

It's not the blowing of the wind that determines your destination, it's the set of the sail.

— Jim Rohn

High school is a constant flood of choices: which friends to hang out with, how much to study for a test, what to do on a Friday night. Navigating all this requires discernment, which is one of the most powerful skills you can develop.

Think of discernment as your inner compass. It's the quiet voice inside you that helps you tell the difference between true north—the direction that aligns with your goals and values—and all the other directions that might seem fun or easy at the moment but will ultimately lead you off course.

Developing this inner compass helps you:

- **See beyond the surface:** To understand the potential consequences of a choice before you make it.
- **Filter out the noise:** To differentiate between what is genuinely good for your growth and what is just a distraction.

- **Trust your gut:** To make decisions that feel right and resonate with the person you want to become.

Improving your discernment isn't just about getting through high school; it's about building a reliable guidance system for your entire life. It ensures that the choices you make today are leading you toward a future you'll be proud of.

Chapter 69: Success and Happiness Leave Clues

Observe the successful person. Study their ways. Then do likewise.

— A common business proverb

Anthony Robbins is a well-known author and motivational speaker. His books have sold millions of copies. According to Robbins, "success leaves clues." I want to add to that and say both success and happiness leave clues. When I meet a young person, I can tell how they are doing and how they are feeling by listening to their voice and answers, paying attention to their tone, and observing their body language and eye contact. These four indicators tell me all I need to know. People watching is an intriguing pastime, something that often sparks both curiosity and reflection. In airports, crowded malls, or vibrant public spaces, observing others can be an enlightening experience.

Think about what is obvious when someone is happy. People almost always respond similarly to some degree. Think about people you see who leave clues of success. The clues of success are slight, subtle differences that people demonstrate daily, separating them from the average and moving them toward excellence in all that they do.

However, remember that it's all a matter of choice. You must start acting in a successful manner before you can become successful. Your habits, the way you treat people, your energy, and your positive mindset stack up and are a choice. Excellence is a choice, a daily choice. It may take a while to adjust to higher standards, but eventually, you will no longer even remember your old standards of average. Then, you can start demonstrating and leaving clues about what success and happiness truly mean.

Chapter 70: How to Get What You Want

You can have everything in life you want if you will just help enough other people get what they want.

— Zig Ziglar

When I was younger and new to the workforce, I read a book about how to get what you want. It offered some excellent ideas and insights on how to succeed in life and work. I was excited because it might be a way to get ahead very quickly. I don't recall the title, as it was over 20 years ago, but the big idea has stuck with me since I finished reading the book. We all wonder how to achieve what we want, especially when we are young and inexperienced. Modern norms expect us to outdo others on our way up the ladder, viewing them as competitors in a dog-eat-dog world.

However, the book's profound impact guided my career toward a different path. Instead of trying to take what you want, help your supervisors get what they want. In other words, rather than being selfish, be selfless and supportive, and you will ultimately achieve your own goals. Putting this idea into practice, I viewed my role in education as helping my principal create an excellent school environment and maintain high learning standards. I would set my ego aside and complete what needed to be done, regardless of whether it fell within my job description or not. I would help custodial staff, playground staff, or anyone else who needed it. This collaborative approach is not just a buzzword—it's the key to success and makes you an integral part of a team. Being a collaborative worker is not just about getting the job done; it's about feeling valued and essential to the group's success.

How does this apply to a high school student? You can act like your teacher is your supervisor and do what you can to help support the best class experience. It may sound corny, but it will make a difference and make you different. Arrive on time, be prepared, sit near the front, ask a question at least four times a week, and complete all your homework. You would be an exceptional individual who consistently makes a positive contribution and sets a great example. How about asking if you understand the material and if any students in class could use some extra help? What does that say about you? It doesn't get attention, but that's who you are and that's what you do. Remember, setting a positive example is not just about your actions; it's about the influence you have on others and the responsibility that comes with it. Your actions have the power to inspire and influence others, and that's a responsibility you should embrace.

Chapter 71: Be There Before You Get There

I skate to where the puck is going to be, not where it has been.

— Wayne Gretzky

How can you be anywhere before you arrive? No, we are not directly discussing time travel, but we are still talking about being in a place before you arrive. How can that happen? The average person in middle school and high school is looking at today, tomorrow, next week, and maybe next month. Although the only thing that exists is the current moment you're living in this very minute. One way to be prepared before you arrive is to start planning and looking ahead to your future, doing your best to create a clear vision of who you want to be and where you want to go.

As you progress through high school, start thinking ahead. You can always change your plan. The average person has minimal short-term vision. These are the simple steps you need to create and live in a way that allows you to be genuinely present before you arrive. There are no guarantees in your life. One thing is for sure: If you think, train, and do things like everyone else, you will be like everyone else.

Visualization is a powerful tool. By starting to see yourself daily achieving your goals and dreams, you are taking control of your future. Remember, everything happens twice—first in your mind, then in reality.

Developing the right mindset is crucial. You need to start thinking and acting like a person who has achieved the goals you have set. Trust yourself and cultivate an attitude of expecting success from the hard work you're putting in and will continue to put in, daily, to achieve your goal.

Creating an action plan is key. What are you willing to do to get moving in the direction you desire? Write a weekly plan or a monthly plan. Post the goals on the mirror so you see them daily. Keep in mind that your plan will evolve as you move forward. Are you willing to give up phone time, get up earlier, or stay up later? You have time; it's a matter of priorities and how you use that time.

Time is valuable, so use it wisely. One of the key motivators is sharing your goals and plans with others. The more people you tell, the more supported and accountable you are. Most people don't tell anyone, so they have no obligation to follow up. I humbly told many people I was planning to write a book, so I would keep moving forward at all times. It works—try it.

I wrote this chapter to help you be prepared before you arrive and to support you as you move forward in pursuing opportunities, such as the choir, dance team, sports team, and other endeavors that may come your way. You can start working toward your goals today.

Chapter 72: The Power of a Mentor

Be more concerned with your character than your reputation, because your character is what you really are, while your reputation is merely what others think you are.

— John Wooden

Have you considered finding a mentor? If you can, find one; don't go through life without one. Most young people don't actively seek a mentor, but you can change that. You can ask

 someone to be your mentor. I look for young people who are truly listening when I talk to them, trying to support and help in their journey. I then try to connect with them. If it's a match, I'm all in. If they are not interested, I sadly move on. A mentor is different from your family. A mentor's role is to guide, support, and offer wisdom. I support young people with books, conversation, and an optimistic view of the genuine value they have in the world. They need to see how amazing they are and be prepared for the best life and version of themselves.

When I was young, I had no idea I needed a mentor. I would have put myself at Level 1 consciousness. Is it a pride issue to think you don't need a mentor, or just a lack of personal awareness? I would encourage you to try it for a while and see the difference it makes. Remember, we can all learn from one another. I now find it my life's calling to walk alongside young people. I don't judge them, tell them what to do, work behind their back, break their trust, or try to be overbearing. I find great joy in being something I needed so desperately as a young person. I think growing up is exciting, but it is also harder these days.

Phones are the most significant change in social dynamics for young people. It has made their lives more challenging, but because they have never lived without it, they are unaware of the difference. Phones have also added some excellent benefits to life, but the challenges can outweigh the benefits. The challenges have increased with the phone and all its capabilities, which can lead you astray, making a mentor even more necessary.

One of my greatest joys in life is walking with young people in their lives. It means the world to me, and I treasure it. I will do my best to be unconditionally helpful. See if you can find a mentor. Ask someone, and most likely they would be honored; you have nothing to lose and everything to gain. The joy and fulfillment of mentorship are something you can look forward to, and it will inspire and guide you in your life.

Chapter 73: Which School Day Is the Most Important?

*Doing the best at this moment puts you in
the best place for the next moment.*

— Oprah Winfrey

I frequently ask students to identify the school day they deem most important throughout the year. I receive a variety of responses, ranging from the first day to the major test day and often the last day. The truth is, every day is essential. Each one has played a role in shaping who you are today.

Progress is a continuous pursuit. We often think a significant test is the most critical moment. However, we should also

consider other pivotal experiences. A difficult conversation with a teacher, for instance, can completely turn your year around. It can leave you feeling more optimistic and empowered.

Countless moments influence us, and it's essential to recognize every day as a component of our growth. This perspective emphasizes the educational process, where grades are merely the outcome. It's within the process that both minor and significant developments occur. Some days may appear better than others, yet they all leave their mark.

Have you ever thought that you might have overlooked a pivotal moment that could have changed your life because you weren't fully engaged or present at that time? You and I will never know if that has happened, but be on the lookout. Don't underestimate each day or take any day for granted; as subtle shifts occur, they may lead you far from your previous path toward a more refined version of yourself. Therefore, continue to adjust your anchor habits, and gradually the world will shift toward a better version of itself for you.

Chapter 74: The End of the School Year Is a Character Test

It is our choices, Harry, that show what we truly are, far more than our abilities.

— J.K. Rowling

I always find it interesting when some students change their behavior as the school year comes to a close. Everyone can feel it when a countdown begins, and people start to reflect on the year, looking forward to new challenges in their lives. It could be a summer job, a trip, off to college, or spending more time with friends.

I offer this to students: You might be very excited to be leaving for the summer, but the end of the year is a character test for you. The challenge is to finish with courtesy and respect toward all, because that is who you are. You may witness a lack of respect and helpfulness in the last few weeks, as some students believe that teachers can't do anything to them because they are leaving. In truth, nobody ever wanted to do anything to them, so stay the course and keep focusing on your journey and character development, regardless of what day it is in school. It's a test—pass it and leave a legacy of gratitude.

Section G: Actions in Your Community and Relationships

While strategic action can propel you toward your personal goals, your success is ultimately shared with others. The strategies for individual achievement must be balanced with how you interact within your community and with your relationships. This section focuses on putting your mindset into action when interacting with others—from taking responsibility as a leader to offering a genuine apology and learning how to belong.

Chapter 75: The Leader Takes the Blame

The leader must own everything in their world. There is no one else to blame.

— Jocko Willink

A powerful lesson on leadership comes from retired Navy SEAL commander Jocko Willink's book, *Extreme Ownership*. He recounts a tragic mission in Ramadi, Iraq, where a "friendly fire" incident led to the death of one of his soldiers and the injury of others. In the chaos of battle, his own troops had mistakenly fired on each other.

During the investigation, there were plenty of available excuses: the complexity of urban warfare, communication breakdowns, or simple human error under immense pressure. It would have been easy to blame the circumstances or other individuals.

Instead, when Willink stood before his superiors, he did the most difficult and courageous thing a leader can do. He took complete responsibility. He stated simply that as the commander, he was to blame for everything that happened. He didn't make excuses or point fingers. He owned the failure, knowing it could end his career. This act of "extreme ownership" didn't just demonstrate his integrity; it set a standard for his entire team.

That story raises a question for all of us: How do we react when things go wrong? It's human nature to look for someone else to blame. But true character is revealed when you choose to take responsibility, especially when it's hard. By owning your mistakes and outcomes, you build trust and earn respect. Willink put his career on the line to prove a simple point: A true leader takes the blame.

How would you have handled that situation? It is easy to blame others when things don't go well. It can be challenging to accept responsibility, even when you feel a situation is beyond your control. I encourage you to take 100 percent responsibility for yourself and everything you do. This will build respect and integrity. It's challenging, but it reveals who you truly are. Jocko put his whole career on the line because he was a leader, and his actions showed it.

Owning everything will work in your favor and make you a leader in both good and challenging times.

As a coach, I have significantly shifted my own mindset. If we play well, I give all the credit to the players. If we don't perform well, I tell the team that I could have done a better job preparing them. I own it now; I used to blame other people. If you want to step up and grow as a leader of character, take 100 percent responsibility for everything with your name attached to it. Others will perceive your avoidance of ownership and will work against you. Owning everything will work in your favor and make you a leader in both good and challenging times.

Chapter 76: The Art of a Real Apology

An apology is the superglue of life. It can repair just about anything.

— Lynn Johnston

Saying you're sorry about something demonstrates a great deal of personal strength, character, and ownership of your behavior. It's a very mature thing to do and reflects a caring attitude and responsibility for a choice we made that was not our best. Our society does not exhibit remorseful behavior overall, as we often blame circumstances or others for our poor decisions, which we justify in our minds as reasons not to apologize.

For whatever reason, I still struggle with apologizing and taking responsibility sometimes, too. We often feel that apologizing is a sign of weakness. Here are some reasons to apologize with sincerity: you have caused harm or distress, you have made a mistake, or you have offended someone. You want to show empathy or acknowledge someone's pain, preserve a relationship, avoid overstepping a boundary, or you have inconvenienced someone. All you need to say is, "I am sorry for it, and it will not happen again." Words like "my bad" or "sorry, bro" lack sincerity and feel like the easy way out. A genuine apology includes a commitment to prevent the situation from happening again. You and I are going to make mistakes.

Own it, apologize, and move on. Don't hang on to guilt if you have done the best you can to fix it and sincerely apologized for whatever needed to be fixed. Don't apologize too quickly, as it may seem insincere. Look the person you're apologizing to in the eye. After you apologize, listen to their response, if any, and refrain from defending yourself. You say, "I understand."

When I was a teacher, I would apologize to a student if I didn't handle a situation very well. It was usually my tone that I apologized for, because I was not speaking respectfully. Having my standards held me accountable, despite being in a position of authority. I needed to set an example, not say one thing and then do another. I focused on living what I asked others to be. The best way to prevent being in these situations is to focus on daily anchor habits that put you in a position to feel and do your best. Everything in your life is interconnected, so take ownership of your actions and do your best.

Your One-Degree Shift

- If there's a small mistake you've made recently (forgot to reply to a text or were short with a sibling), offer a simple, genuine apology without making an excuse.

Chapter 77: See the Person, Not the Problem

If we have no peace, it is because we have forgotten that we belong to each other.

— Mother Teresa

As you grow and move through life at what will seem a faster pace, I ask that you look at people in a different light—a light that demonstrates you have a big heart. Everyone you come in contact with each day is someone's son, daughter, mother, or father. Why does this matter? Because if you look at each person as part of a family, they become much more human to you. When we think of our own family, we become more compassionate, tolerant, and forgiving. Your patience and kindness will mean a lot to them, even if they don't seem to deserve it.

If everyone started to act with this type of compassionate heart, the impact would be huge in our schools and communities. There is too much dehumanizing of others in the world when they are different, don't understand, or take too much time in line. However, a trying moment does not justify your heart becoming rigid and intolerant, which is easy to do; I have done it and still have to fight it off at times.

This is where your standards come in. You have standards of care for others—that is who you're choosing to become. When you perform a helpful act of support or kindness, expect nothing in return. I challenge myself all the time to help others without expectation, because wanting something back is my ego talking. I want to be valuable and selfless. A selfless heart has the power to bring hope and optimism to our communities through acts of grace, tolerance, and compassion.

Chapter 78: You Teach People How to Treat You

No one can make you feel inferior without your consent.

— Eleanor Roosevelt

Have you ever considered what you allow from people toward you, or how you stick up for yourself? It's interesting that when we are young, we tend to avoid conflict, yet we always feel better when a dispute is resolved. We often allow behaviors from others and blame them, but do nothing to set boundaries, share with them that we do not appreciate something they do, or address the general treatment we receive.

Here's the hard truth: By not addressing it, you're effectively allowing the issue to persist. You may lack the confidence to address it or be concerned that it could exacerbate the situation. However, remember that setting boundaries is not just about others; it's also about respecting yourself. You need to stand up for yourself, and the sooner you learn to be active toward and fair with how people treat you, the sooner you will gain the skills for future conflicts that may occur in the workplace. You can do it; everything you work on today, this week, next month, or next year will serve as a valuable lesson to guide you as you continue to grow and become a better version of yourself. Stand up for yourself in a kind and caring way, and teach people how to treat you; it's an excellent form of self-respect.

Chapter 79: Taking Compliments

Accepting a compliment is a learned skill. It's gracious and kind. It's also a gift to the person who is giving it.

— Unknown

When someone compliments you about who you are or what you're doing, it's crucial to acknowledge it. An effortless "Thank you; I appreciate it, and thank you for letting me know" can go a long way. I've noticed that when I share a compliment, many people either don't respond or downplay what they're being complimented about. This can discourage others from complimenting you. Remember, people notice and appreciate your gratitude, so be gracious and acknowledge their kind words with sincerity. It's that simple.

Chapter 80: Stop Talking and Stop Digging

It is better to keep your mouth closed and let people think you are a fool than to open it and remove all doubt.

— Mark Twain

You're going to make mistakes. It's a natural part of growing up. But one of the most important skills you can learn is what to do *after* you've messed up, especially when a parent, teacher, or coach is upset with you. The best advice is this: stop talking and start listening. I hear people all the time trying to rationalize or justify their poor choices, and they are just making a challenging situation worse by continuing to talk. Stop talking and digging a bigger hole for yourself.

Try to focus and understand the person in charge of handling the problem. They may be

speaking in a strong and intense tone. They are upset about the situation. When people are upset or emotional, they are not in a good place to listen. Realize this and once again be in charge of yourself and just listen. Your talking is a poor choice in these moments because they are upset with you and working to help you, although it may not feel like it. You may not like the way they are handling the situation, but keep your cool and stay focused as a good listener. The respect you show is the first step in healing and dealing with the issue. Read the room, and if the person is upset with you or the situation, just be a respectful listener and seek to understand. Wait until they ask you what happened or why you did what you did. Your time to talk will come.

Chapter 81: The Courage to Belong

True belonging doesn't require you to change who you are; it requires you to be who you are.

— Brené Brown

Who do you have to become, or what authentic part of yourself do you have to change to fit in? Do you have to act a certain way, dress a certain way, drink alcohol, use poor language, do sexual things you don't want to do, just to have a boyfriend or girlfriend? Do you have to not like a particular person or group, be disrespectful to others, or make some other compromising choice to fit in with a group? That is a painful compromise.

I know that as a younger person, I was a follower and lacked the courage to walk my walk at times. I often chose to try to fit in. I wish I hadn't, as I've grown older, and sometimes I still feel disappointed when I look back. I know I shouldn't, but I still struggle with it at times. The only person I was hurting was myself at the end of the day. But I also learned from those mistakes, and that's the beauty of life- we can always learn and grow.

Belonging is being accepted for who you are; fitting in means compromising to be part of something.

— Brené Brown

I discuss it now to help others learn and grow, and to consider avoiding the pitfalls of compromising to fit in. I challenge you to think it through and grow stronger within yourself, making changes that allow you to be yourself and start thinking about belonging instead. Belonging is being accepted for who you are; fitting in means compromising to be part of something. Seeking to belong might mean changing your social group or even walking alone. I wish I had walked alone instead of trying so hard to fit in where I did not belong in the first place. Where are you currently walking?

Section H: Actions for a Resilient Mindset

Acting with integrity in your daily relationships is crucial, but your mindset is truly forged in moments of adversity. How do you act when faced with unfairness, failure, or circumstances beyond your control? The following chapters focus on building resilience through action. We'll explore the mindsets of survivors, the power of grit, and how to find joy even when conditions aren't perfect.

Chapter 82: The Mindset of a Survivor

I am not what happened to me,
I am what I choose to become.

— Attributed to Carl Jung

Arunima Sinha was a national volleyball player with a bright future. That future was violently derailed in 2011, when she was pushed from a moving train by robbers, an attack that led to the amputation of her left leg.

While lying in her hospital bed, surrounded by pity and an uncertain future, Sinha made a decision that defied all logic. She refused to be seen as a victim. Instead of focusing on what she had lost, she set a goal so audacious it seemed impossible: she would become the first female amputee to climb Mount Everest.

The real Everest is inside you.

— Arunima Sinha

She endured excruciating pain during her training, learning to climb with a prosthetic leg. In 2013, just two years after her life-altering accident, she stood on top of the world.

Arunima Sinha's story is the ultimate example of choosing your own narrative. She looked at the worst moment of her life and decided it would not be her ending, but the beginning of her true greatness. Her mindset teaches us that we are not defined by what happens to us, but by the goals we set in response. [Story paraphrased from Wikipedia contributors, "Arunima Sinha," *Wikipedia, The Free Encyclopedia,* https://en.wikipedia.org/w/index.php?title=Arunima_Sinha&oldid=1316726274 (accessed October 21, 2025).]

Chapter 83: The Single Most Important Word for Your Future

Grit is passion and perseverance for very long-term goals. Grit is having stamina. Grit is sticking with your future, day in, day out, not just for the week, not just for the month, but for years, and working really hard to make that future a reality.

— Angela Duckworth

There is one quality that matters more than talent, intelligence, or luck when it comes to long-term success. It's called grit. Angela Duckworth, a professor and researcher, defines grit as the combination of passion and perseverance. Gritty people are relentless. They don't quit. Her research is fascinating because it proves that success isn't about having the best natural ability; it's about having the most determination. In her book, *Grit*, she shows that the candidates who survive the grueling "Beast Week" at West Point and the students who win the Scripps National Spelling Bee are not always the most talented—they are the ones with the most grit.

When I look back at my struggling start in school, I realize now that my superpower was grit. I didn't know it then, but it's what carried me. I faced academic challenges, but I was passionate and persevered to attend college, earn a master's degree, and play collegiate basketball. I often stumbled, but I always got back up and kept moving forward.

I want you to adopt a mindset anchored in grit. Know that there will be bumps in the road, but you can remain relentless and unstoppable. The key is growing it daily. Start with these simple steps: set long-term goals and break them down into smaller tasks; maintain a positive attitude; and, most importantly, learn from your failures instead of letting them hold you back.

Remain focused and consistent each day—that is what grit looks like in real life. There will be tough days and people who doubt you, but they are only temporary slowdowns. Learn more about grit, talk about it with others, and encourage it in your friends. Make grit a core part of your mindset, starting today.

Your One-Degree Shift

- The next time you feel frustrated and want to quit a task (homework, a video game level, etc.), use the 2-Minute Rule: Stay with it for just two more minutes.

Chapter 84: Conditions Do Not Determine Your Attitude

We cannot choose our external circumstances, but we can always choose how we respond to them.

— Epictetus

Viktor Frankl, a Holocaust survivor from World War II, was imprisoned in four concentration camps during the war. His book, *Man's Search for Meaning,* has been a must-read for much of the 20th and 21st centuries. As a neurologist and a psychiatrist, he had a unique insight into people, which he shared through his influential book. In these camps, he witnessed and experienced unimaginable suffering, starvation, and death. Yet, amidst these horrors, he noticed a remarkable phenomenon: Some prisoners, despite their dire circumstances, managed to maintain a sense of hope and dignity. This stark contrast between the extreme conditions and the prisoners' maintained hope and dignity is a testament to the power of mindset.

I would like to break down a quote from the book regarding your mindset, as it shares insights from the most horrific conditions and treatments a person can endure. His experiences and observations shed light on the profound influence of mindset on outcomes, even in the most extreme circumstances.

Everything can be taken from a man but one thing: the last of the human freedoms—to choose one's attitude in any given set of circumstances, to choose one's way.

— Viktor Frankl

In the quote, Viktor Frankl argues that people always have a choice about their attitude, even in the most dire conditions, as he experienced firsthand. This concept of choice is at the heart of Frankl's philosophy, underlining the freedom and responsibility individuals have in shaping their attitudes. People were starving to death, and yet they still gave away their last piece of bread to help others try to survive. Think about that power of choice for a moment. It's difficult to fathom what we would do in such circumstances. What an incredible will of choice and spirit. It was a freedom that can never be taken away. Conditions refer to external circumstances, yet a choice is always available in your mind toward your circumstances. This is a powerful quote, as we often find ways to complain or use conditions as a way to blame our present attitude. Frankl saw firsthand the power of choice. Remember this when you think you're having a challenging time.

Focus on what you can control. Your attitude is that choice of response. Prisoners of these camps had everything taken away, and people did everything humanly possible to remove their dignity. As Viktor Frankl observed, your attitude is a freedom and a responsibility to yourself and your growth. It's a call to accountability, a reminder that we are responsible for our attitudes and the impact they have on our lives and on those we encounter.

I would also strongly encourage you to read *Man's Search for Meaning*, as it delves into what people are truly capable of becoming or not becoming in the toughest of times. Your attitude is always your choice. Circumstances may be challenging, but you have the option to determine your attitude toward them. Always keep this in mind, as it's a mindset that requires constant attention.

Chapter 85: The Science of Gratitude

It is not joy that makes us grateful;
it is gratitude that makes us joyful.

— David Steindl-Rast

When you're feeling down about yourself and things aren't going the way you'd like, consider doing a small act of kindness for others. This could be as easy as writing a thank-you note to a colleague or helping a friend with a task. We can fall into a downward cycle of self-reflection, and self-pity can start to seep in.

Eventually, it may pour into our mindset, and we will have a full-on pity party. You may have it rough, but I always ask myself, compared to what or whom? Making gratitude a daily habit helps avoid and alleviate self-pity. Gratitude can help you avoid focusing on any lack of abundance or what is wrong in your life. Everyone has struggles in their life.

Making gratitude a daily habit helps avoid and alleviate self-pity.

Acts of appreciation can help boost your feelings of positive emotions and increase your levels of dopamine and serotonin. What are dopamine and serotonin? Dopamine is released when you experience something pleasurable. It's a "feel-good" neurotransmitter. Serotonin is also a neurotransmitter, and its primary role includes maintaining mood balance, promoting feelings of well-being, and contributing to happiness. When you practice gratitude, your brain recognizes the positive experience and releases dopamine. This reinforces your behavior and increases the likelihood that you will repeat it. Serotonin, on the other hand, is released when you feel significant. By expressing gratitude, you acknowledge the importance of others in your life, which can lead to an increase in serotonin levels. Both dopamine and serotonin have distinct functions, but they also work together to maintain a bodily balance.

Gratitude releases neurotransmitters, including dopamine, serotonin, oxytocin, and endorphins, which is why it is essential to acknowledge your appreciation and perform small acts of kindness daily. They will lift you and cancel any potential pity parties you may be having or are planning for the week ahead, but you don't know it yet. Consider shifting your mindset toward appreciating others and the small things you can do to show it, and the rewards you will receive as your body releases chemicals to support a good mood. You can do it!

Chapter 86: Beyond First-World Problems

Some people complain because roses have thorns; I am grateful that thorns have roses.

— Alphonse Karr

If you're reading this book, you're likely sitting in a reasonably safe location. Why do I mention that? In this country, despite its challenges, there is no better opportunity for a good quality of life anywhere else in the world.

It's always interesting to hear people complain about their situations. Complaining easily becomes a habit that people often normalize and simply do because others join in and fuel the fire, allowing it to continue burning. I move away from complainers, period. I can find complainers anywhere. They are energy suckers. However, here's the thing: You have the power to change your perspective and break the cycle of complaining. You have the power to focus on the abundance of privileges you have and be grateful for them.

When I hear people complaining, I usually ask myself quietly, "Compared to what?" You have an excellent chance at a great education. I am not dismissing the need for people to share frustrations about health issues, low-income, family dynamics, and problems that are beyond challenging to handle. It is essential to express and address your feelings.

Did you shower with hot water today? Did you get breakfast? Did you have many clothes to choose from today? Did you have a cell phone to charge? Did you work on your computer last night? Did you watch cable TV? You get the idea; a lot of people are blessed with so much. We have apps that will do almost everything for us, and yet people still complain. Realize there will always be rainy days, high traffic, lots of homework, late nights at work, and more. But if you shift your perspective and focus on gratitude, you'll find that even on those rainy days, you have so much to be thankful for.

When you hear people complaining, ask yourself in your inner voice, "Compared to what?" and don't join in. Sharing your feelings is very healthy, but complaining does not create an optimistic mindset that keeps you energized and has a positive impact on those around you.

Chapter 87: Fun, Happiness, and Joy: What's the Difference?

Joy does not simply happen to us. We have to choose joy and keep choosing it every day.

— Henri Nouwen

We often talk about being happy and having fun. We chase these feelings, thinking they're the ultimate goal. But there's a more profound, more powerful feeling that truly defines a good life: **joy**. Understanding the difference is a game-changer.

Think of it like this:

- **Fun** is like eating a candy bar. It's a quick, sweet rush that comes from an activity—a party, a game, a good movie. It's great, but it's temporary.
- **Happiness** is like having a delicious meal with friends. It's a feeling of satisfaction that comes from good circumstances—getting a good grade, spending time with people you like. It's terrific, but it often depends on external things going right.

- **Joy**, however, is like learning to cook for yourself. It's a deep, internal feeling of peace and fulfillment that you cultivate over time. It doesn't depend on a specific activity or circumstance. It's the quiet confidence you feel at the end of a tough school year, knowing you grew through the challenges. Joy is what sustains you through both the good times and the bad.

Joy is the feeling that lasts. It encompasses all the ups and downs and recognizes that a meaningful life is built, not just experienced.

As you look back on your life, you'll have many fun moments and happy days. But the goal is to seek joy. Joy is the feeling that lasts. It encompasses all the ups and downs and recognizes that a meaningful life is built, not just experienced.

Chapter 88: Rethinking Fairness

Equality is giving everyone a shoe. Equity is giving everyone a shoe that fits.

— Dr. Naheed Dosani

If you are reading this book, you're among the privileged, believe it or not. Why would I say that? Because approximately 62 percent of the world's population lives on less than 10 dollars a day. You likely spent more than that to read this book. When I was younger, I always thought fairness meant equality. In kindergarten, if there was a cookie and both students wanted some, you would split it in half. That was equal.

Fairness is about getting what you need, not necessarily what you want or what someone else has.

I hope you will consider a new perspective on fairness that I have found to be a more effective way of looking at the world: Fundamentally, understand that fair is not the same as equal. The only thing everyone gets equally is time. Each day, you get 86,400 seconds. How you use that time is up to you. I am not talking about voting rights, equal pay for equal work, or equal opportunity for qualified candidates, or any other issues like these. Fairness is about getting what you need, not necessarily what you want or what someone else has.

Why should we look at fairness in life this way? Because the takeaway is that many of us have an abundance of everything. We often have many choices to make when we start our day, from what to eat and wear to what to pack for lunch. Keep in mind that it's not the case for everybody.

We live in a world of abundance in this country, in both material goods and opportunity. So, when it comes to being fair, we all have a head start; the question is not whether it's equal, but what is fair? Fair compared to what? Ask someone who has to walk three miles for clean water what "fair" means, and you'll get a very different answer.

Consider this version of fairness whenever possible, and remember how fortunate you are. When I think this way, I prioritize other people first and myself second. Fifteen minutes from now, how it all went down will make little difference in my life. This is why I wonder about why I get stuck on what is fair. Fair is not equal.

Chapter 89: Who You Are Is Not What You Do

Be yourself; everyone else is already taken.

— Anonymous

"Who are you?" is a fascinating question to ask young people. When I was young, I never even thought about this concept. Even later in life, I still had it all wrong. Then, I came across a book called *What Drives Winning* by Brett Ledbetter. Brett points out in the book that character is who you are, and the process of showing and developing it is what you do. An example from his book is an NBA coach asking his 11 players, "Would you rather play in the NBA or have good character?" Nine of the 11 players chose to play in the NBA. According to Ledbetter, "Here's what's interesting: Playing in the NBA is *what* you do. Having good character is *who you are*."

When asked who they are, a young person will almost always start with what they do: "I am a student, I play a sport or an instrument, and I play video games with my friends"; and it continues with things that they do. That is not who you are. **Think about it for a second.** If I were asked who I am, I would say I'm a teacher, a family man, a coach, and so on. When I retired, I struggled with my identity because I had always been a teacher, a coach, and a family man. I suddenly didn't have a good answer, not even within my understanding of who I was. Soon after I retired, I read Brett's book, and I finally found out who I am and what I still want to become. I am caring, helpful, hardworking, honest, and giving. I continue to strive to become more honorable, practice daily gratitude, demonstrate courage, and show greater kindness and compassion. That is who I want to be! It's a daily work in progress, but my passion drives my level of determination and pursuit. Who are you aiming to be? Do not confuse it with what you do.

Your One-Degree Shift

- Write down three words that describe *who you are* (e.g., "curious," "resilient," "kind") that have nothing to do with your grades, sports, or hobbies.

- The next time you talk to a friend, ask them about something they are passionate about or what they've learned recently, instead of just asking about their performance in a game or on a test.

Section I: The Practical Toolkits

Building a resilient mindset gives you the strength to withstand life's storms. This final section provides the practical details for building the ship itself. Here, we move from concepts to concrete systems—the specific toolkits for executive functioning and financial freedom that can serve as the operating system for your entire life. These are the tools that will help you execute your plan and truly defy average.

Chapter 90: Executive Functioning Toolkit

For every minute spent in organizing, an hour is earned.

— Attributed to Benjamin Franklin

This chapter is about the small hinges that swing big doors. The ideas presented here may seem easy, but they represent the one-degree shifts we discussed in the Preface. Consistently writing down your homework or organizing your folders isn't just about being neat; it's a daily habit that compounds over time, steering you toward a future where you're in control, prepared, and confident.

Write It Down

- It's key to write down all your homework, upcoming tests, and quizzes in the same  place and do it consistently for each class. Even if there's no homework, jot down "no HW" for each class. This practice builds a habit of organization and accountability and gives you a sense of control over your academic responsibilities. Find a method and a place (in a computer doc, a spreadsheet, Google Docs, a notebook, etc.) where you can do it in less than 30 seconds at the end of every class. Do not leave class without writing it down. Remember, what seems easy to do is also easy not to do; do it so you don't have to remember it. This control is key to your academic success, and it should empower you to achieve your goals.

Folder for Success

- Whether it's a physical folder or digital ones on your laptop, color-code them for each class. On the inside sleeves, write "To Be Done," and on another inside sleeve, write "Completed." This simple yet effective method not only keeps your materials organized but also provides a visual cue of what needs to be done and what has already been completed, making you feel more prepared and in control of your academic tasks. This preparedness will boost your confidence in handling your academic workload, and it should make you feel more confident. The "folder for success" method keeps your materials organized and provides a **visual cue** of your progress, making you feel more prepared and in control.

Where You Sit Matters

- Where you sit in the classroom can significantly impact your learning. Aim to be seated in the front third of the class. This position allows you to hear the teacher and see the board without any obstruction, minimizing distractions. While sitting with friends may be comforting, it often leads to distraction and concentration issues. Be honest with your teacher and request to be moved. They will respect your commitment to learning. Consider leaving your phone in your locker to avoid temptation. Remember, where you sit matters for your focus and engagement.

Know the Goal of Every Class

- Never leave a class without knowing what the learning outcome was supposed to be. Learning outcomes are the specific knowledge, skills, and attitudes that you should have acquired by the end of the class. For instance, in a history class, the learning outcomes include understanding a specific event, writing a coherent essay, and developing a critical attitude toward historical sources. Understanding these outcomes helps you stay focused during the class and guides your study sessions. If you do leave class without knowing the learning outcomes, it will just add to your confusion when you try to catch up. Learning a little new information is much easier than learning a lot of new material in a short time. Too many people let the unlearned class sessions accumulate until it becomes emotionally overwhelming. They essentially give up, and their grade suffers; their stress level increases, and they are unprepared for that part of the final exam. The lack of understanding also becomes apparent on the semester's final exam. It dings you twice. Take control of your learning outcomes to be a responsible student, and you should feel more accountable.

Consistency Wins

- Just as going to bed at the same time helps establish a consistent sleeping pattern, doing your homework at the same time helps build a habit of consistency, too. I encourage students to start with 10 minutes of their most challenging class's homework first. Why? Two reasons: First, most students tend to put it off until last because, emotionally, it doesn't feel good, and we don't feel powerful, so we avoid it as long as possible. Then, we wind up being tired, distracted, or making excuses. Second, our willpower tends to wane as the day passes. This is why people do so well and then struggle later in the day; emotionally, with their diet, and with starting and doing homework.

Look Often, Even If You Have No Idea

- It may not be the most exciting part of your day, but it's beneficial to study your most challenging classes for 10-15 minutes each day, even if you don't understand what's going on with the material. Allow your brain to organize over time. Your brain will try to figure it out. It's like a puzzle; even if you don't understand the material now, if you keep looking at it, it will eventually snap into place and connect in your brain, leading to a deeper understanding. If you never look at it, even if you don't understand the material, it will never have a chance to snap into place. However, you're not giving it a chance if you don't look at it because it doesn't exist in your brain, as you don't even have a recollection of what it is. We, as people, try to connect information that we have in our brains, but do not yet understand, in the early moments of seeing, hearing, reading, or experiencing it. We try to put things together all the time that we see, hear, read, and experience. Then one day, magically, we figure it out; and poof—it all comes together. That only happens when you trust the process and stay the course. If you choose to never look at your challenging class material, you can guarantee failure. Don't blame the material; blame the process you deliberately decided not to do and the lack of commitment to yourself. Anything you do not learn directly affects you.

Plan Your Morning Success

- First, the night before every school day, create a short list of tasks (things to do or remember to do) on a sticky note to get started on after eating breakfast and getting dressed for school. Place it in a visible location, like on your breakfast bowl or coffee cup, or wherever you will see it in the morning. This list would include any questions you need to ask a teacher, any homework you need to submit, and appointments for extra help or contact with someone you need to schedule for the start of your day. Secondly, prepare for your morning, which allows you to execute a plan without having to create one on the fly. Do tasks like laying out your clothes, preparing your breakfast (including silverware and cups or plates), packing your bag or backpack, and gathering any other essentials you might need—all in preparation for tomorrow.

Preparing the night before eliminates the stress of morning decisions. When you wake up, start with a glass of water and avoid checking your phone or drinking caffeine for the first 30 minutes, as both can increase your cortisol levels. Why should you not look at your phone right away? If you do that, something will catch your attention, or something else will cause stress, making it a very challenging way to leave the house: preoccupied or worried. Your morning plan is to wake up and execute the plan you have set up. No thinking is required for your morning routine; it's all about execution, which will ensure it runs smoothly and leads to a great start to your day.

I hear of too many students trying to figure out what to wear to school, and then they are running late because they cannot find it, so they just skip breakfast because they are in a hurry. That is not the answer. Now, you're going 3-4 hours on an empty stomach; no wonder you cannot stay focused. You have set yourself up to struggle. Failing to plan is planning to fail.

I have been doing what I previously wrote about for 30 years. I make a list every night before I go to sleep, so I don't have to remember anything in the morning. I have a to-do list to get me started when I arrive at school, and I can sleep worry-free. I put my list on my car keys so I don't forget it. Guess how many times I have driven to work without my car keys? You guessed it, zero. I can't drive without them, so I never forget my list.

I also lay out my clothes, breakfast, and book bag on top of the shoes I plan to wear;

that way, I cannot miss a thing on my way out. If you bring lunch each day, prepare it the night before and add it to your list for the next day. Take nothing for granted; set up a morning execution plan. Stress in the morning will not get you off to a great start. It's a choice you can control, and it works. Set yourself up to have a great start to your day. It will take you 10 minutes each night to do it. The better version of you gets to walk out the door in the morning. That is a win-win.

Being Intentional

- You now have a solid fundamental understanding of the distinction between having intentions and being intentional. When it comes to homework, you need to be intentional about your approach. What time are you going to get started? Tell someone, or write it down. I suggest you get a day planner and block out the times so you know the flow of your day.

Remember, your willpower tends to decrease as the day progresses. If you leave your homework until later in the night and decide what to do based on how you're feeling, it will likely not end very consistently or well. Do it early when you have more willpower and brainpower. Also, I will tell you what science tells us: The more people we tell we are going to do something, the more likely we are to do it. Tell family members what time you're going to start your homework. I told many people I was going to write this book. Not to brag, but to hold myself accountable and keep moving forward. I didn't tell everyone, just a few people I respected. Do the same with your homework to build up expectations and deliver on follow-through.

Chunking

- When you have a big project or a big paper due, meet with someone you respect and trust and ask them to break it down with you. What is chunking? Chunking involves breaking down a project into small, manageable pieces to complete it. Here is an example:

Project Topic: Tectonic Plates

Assignment: 6-8 page paper due Feb. 15th

Expectations: Each student will explain and explore where tectonic plates meet and how this impacts the region. Focus on activity, discuss plate boundaries, subduction zones, types of earthquakes, and volcanoes in the area. Include the history of the region you're covering in your project.

If this were your project, you would:

- Map out how many weeks you have before the due date. Total days?

- Determine when, where, and how to obtain resources and when you need them to initiate the project, along with the deadline for receiving your resources.
- Create an outline of what you plan to cover, and set a completion date.
- Set a date to write and complete a rough draft that answers the requirements of the project grading or rubric.
- Maybe have a peer edit to see how your writing and resources are shaping up. Do you have a deadline for this? Set one.
- Take the time to ask the teacher questions about any concerns that are unclear to you.
- Write a final copy of the project a few days before the deadline and review it.
- Fix any final-draft issues after your review and print it a day early, so you're ready to hand it in and avoid printer issues that only sound like excuses when you have had weeks to do something.

The few ideas I have listed here are fundamentals for increasing your agency in school. There is no doubt that people are complex, and executive functioning issues vary from person to person. For some, executive functioning is not an issue at school. For others, like me, it was a significant obstacle to my academic success. I hope you and your caregiver will advocate for support with executive functioning skills at your school if you feel the need for it. You matter, and everything you do or don't do stacks up. Make it happen, cultivate the correct habits, and build the best life you'll live tomorrow.

Homework Time

- Homework success is predicated on building small habits that accumulate, much like the other things we have shared so far. Homework habits should be established when students are young, and then be monitored as they transition into middle school and continue into the first two years of high school. I work with students from all high school grade levels, and there are many reasons homework does not get done. These must be handled in a one-on-one situation.

Here are my suggestions for slowly increasing homework completion. Do your homework in the same place each night. Often, a bedroom is filled with distractions and little accountability. I suggest the kitchen table or an office in the house. Give your phone to a caregiver when you start. If you need to set a timer, please let the caregiver know when it will go off and at what time. Speaking of time, try to do homework at the same time each night, preferably soon after dinner. Do some after that and see how you like it. Focus on one class at a time. Multitasking is shown to be slower than doing one task at a time. I always say to do 10 minutes of your most challenging class and then move on to a different subject, even if you're not done. Why? Because while you're working on the new topic, your brain will be organizing the return to the previous subject, and you will know how and where to pick up and complete it. Spend time on every topic, even on the days of no homework. The information you see helps you retain more, making school easier. Dedicate the time to be dedicated to yourself. The payoff is in the future.

One more idea about homework. Set your phone to go off every 15 minutes, as long as you're not using it and it is not distracting you, once you start your homework. If your 15-minute phone timer is too distracting, consider getting an inexpensive countdown timer with no distracting features and place your phone in another room. Two things will happen if you do it this way. First, reflect on how productively you used your 15 minutes. If it was productive, reset the timer, go another 15 minutes, and review again. Ask yourself what you accomplished. Second, the 15-minute timer will bring you back into focus and limit your daydreaming or doodling to only 15 minutes before the buzzer goes off, getting you back to the task at hand. If you do not use a timer this way, you may doodle or daydream for a long time before something reminds you to regain your focus.

Studying for Tests

- I talk to so many people who plant the wrong seeds all the time. They repeat it and repeat it, yet still get the same stressed-out, poor test results. They then blame themselves for not being smart, or the material for being too hard, or the teacher for not doing their job very well. If you prepare the same way repeatedly without success, it's time to try a new approach.

Here is an example to illustrate everyday high school moments. Suppose you have a math test on Friday. What does the typical student do on Thursday night? They crack open the math book and begin reviewing the unit material covered in the book for the upcoming test. This type of studying routine usually goes one of two ways. Either you go through the material and feel confident that you know it all, or you're prepared for the test tomorrow. You did not plant any doubt seeds in your mind. You feel fine and sleep well in preparation for the math test on Friday.

Now for a more typical response: You crack open the book the night before the test and realize you have a lot of questions and aren't sure about the material. So you plant small doubt seeds in your brain that will be sprouting up very quickly when you lie in bed and start to worry. These doubt seeds will erode your confidence, and you will not do very well on Friday's math test. You planted the seeds that stress you out and cause anxiety because you lost your confidence, and now you have little time to recover. Sleep was a challenge last night as the seeds you planted while studying grew into large, self-doubting trees. Why do we keep planting the same seeds of doubt that disrupt our sleep, create a lack of confidence in our mindset, increase anxiety, and undermine our confidence and personal power? We do this because it's our habit, and we're not sure how to break it.

How about we do something different to break the cycle?

The top row is weekdays.

HW = homework

ST = study time

The middle row represents the traditional approach to test preparation.

The bottom row represents the new way to prepare for tests.

Mon.	Tues.	Wed.	Thurs.	Fri.
HW for math	HW for math	HW for math	ST 2 hours	Math Test
HW for math ST 15 minutes	HW for math ST 15 minutes	HW for math ST 15 minutes	ST 1 hour	Math Test

When you examine the study time, the new test prep method has fewer minutes. If you look at something more often with regularity, your brain processes it more efficiently, and the brain will increase its familiarity with it. If you need to get a drink from a hose, you don't turn the water on full blast, as there is too much coming at you too fast. That is what happens when you try to cram the night before. Your brain becomes saturated very quickly, and then you become concerned about actually knowing it, and doubt seeds are planted. Logically, the more you see and do something, the easier it becomes and the quicker you become proficient in it. Looking at it for a shorter duration, more often, helps the brain absorb it. Another benefit is that if you have questions about the previous material, you have time to get help. Cramming is like getting a drink from a firehose. Too much water (math information) can be taken in too fast by cramming on Thursday, whereas keeping the water pressure low (Monday, Tuesday, and Wednesday) allows you to take in more due to the increased flow rate.

Manage Your Frustration: The 2-Minute Rule

You're going to get stuck. A math problem will feel impossible, or a paragraph won't sound right. In that moment, your brain will scream, "I can't do this!" This is where you lose power. Instead of giving in to frustration, use the 2-Minute Rule: Work on the problem with intense focus for just two more minutes. If you're still stuck after 120 seconds, it's okay to move on to something else and come back later, or mark it down to ask for help. This strategy teaches your brain to push through difficulty without letting frustration take over your entire study session. It's a small act of discipline that builds immense mental toughness.

The 5-Minute Rule: How to Start When You Don't Want To

The hardest part of any task is starting. Procrastination isn't about being lazy; it's about avoiding a feeling of discomfort. The solution is the 5-Minute Rule: Tell yourself you only have to work on that challenging assignment for five minutes. Anyone can handle five minutes. Set a timer. Often, that initial push is all you need to break through the resistance and build momentum. And if you still want to stop after five minutes? You can. But you've started, and that's a small win that proves you are in control, not your feelings.

A small win proves you are in control, not your feelings.

Use Your Tech for Good

Your phone can be your biggest distraction or your most powerful tool—it's up to you. Instead of letting it control you, make it work for you.

- **Use the calendar app:** Enter every due date, test date, and project deadline into your phone or computer's calendar, setting reminders for two days in advance.

- **Master the timer:** Use the Pomodoro Technique. Set a timer for 20 minutes of focused work, then take a 5-minute break. This trains your brain to concentrate in short, powerful bursts.

- **Dictate your notes:** Feeling overwhelmed by writing? Use your phone's voice-to-text feature to speak your ideas for an essay. It's often faster and helps get your thoughts flowing. Using your technology intentionally is a massive step in defying average.

Create a "Shutdown Ritual"

Your school day doesn't end when you finish your last homework problem. It ends when you're prepared for the next day. Create a five-minute "shutdown ritual" for the end of your night.

1. **Review your planner/list:** Check what's due tomorrow.

2. **Pack your bag:** Put every completed assignment, folder, and book in your backpack—no more frantic morning searches.

3. **Review your morning plan:** Refer to the sticky note you created for the morning to keep it fresh in your mind. This ritual signals to your brain that the work is done, allowing you to relax fully and sleep more soundly. It ensures that you

walk out the door the next morning feeling prepared and powerful, not stressed and rushed.

Your One-Degree Shift

- Tonight, before you go to bed, lay out your clothes for tomorrow and pack your backpack.

- At the end of each class tomorrow, take 30 seconds to write down your homework in one consistent place.

Chapter 91: A Simple Path to Financial Freedom

Do not save what is left after spending;
instead,
spend what is left after saving.

— Warren Buffett

We've spent this book laying the foundation, cultivating the mindset, and equipping you with the tools for a great life. This final chapter contains a tool that can affect not just you but your entire family for generations to come: a straightforward path to financial freedom. To help you on the long-term journey of defying average, I want to leave you with this final, powerful tool. Let's talk about your future.

A Simple Path to Financial Freedom

I am sure you have thought about how your future will look and what you will be doing for a living. Will you make a lot of money, or will it be a challenge? I am going outside the scope of this book, and I encourage you to conduct further research on this topic. If no one ever tells you about this, or you don't hear about it when you are young, time becomes your enemy. I'd like to share an idea that isn't mine, but I implemented it later in life and am now trying to share it with young people. How can you change your life later on and impact the next generation of family members behind you? As we know, simple is not easy, and easy is not simple.

When you turn 18 to 20 years old and start working at a job where you begin to earn some money, here's how you should prioritize your finances.

1. **Pay your bills:** You may have a cell phone bill, car insurance, and gas for your car, among other expenses. In some cases, you may still live at home and have no expenses. You may also need to save for college. There will be a lot of things vying for the money you earn.
2. **Save:** This is the point where you should save money. The first point is to be responsible, and the second point is to save for your future. Again, your future self will thank you. You can change a

generation by saving a little money each month.

3. **Fun money:** This is the money left over that you get to enjoy life with. You can go to a movie, eat at a restaurant, and more. That will not be as fun as you think. Being poor is not fun, and having no savings greatly increases your stress. Saving some money each month builds confidence and comfort, allowing you to handle the future.

Here's the trap most people fall into: they swap the second and third priorities, putting "fun money" ahead of saving. This is a mistake. Trying to keep up with everyone else and going broke in the process. Don't follow the crowd when spending money. You will feel more powerful if you set your own path of saving. People are going broke trying to look wealthy or successful. It's easy to tell they are not rich and not very successful because that is not what people with money do. They save, invest, and stop trying to impress. Saving and having money brings a sense of peace of mind. Although it does not solve all your problems, it helps alleviate some of them. It can also add to more problems if you don't save.

People are going broke trying to look wealthy or successful.

So what do you do? This isn't to say you must do nothing but work. But when you work more, you tend to spend less because you are working. You work with a purpose to transform the drip of money you make now into a stream, then a river, next a great lake, and finally an ocean. It takes time and consistency, just like many of the things I have discussed.

Disclaimer: I am not a financial expert or advisor. The following suggestions are based on my personal experience. Please conduct your own research or consult with a professional before making any investment decisions. Time is your friend when you start early. The longer you wait to invest, the more you need to invest to catch up.

1. Work or save until you have saved $1,000, which is what you need to open a Roth IRA. A Roth IRA is a retirement savings account that allows your money to grow tax-free. This means you won't pay taxes on your investment gains, which can significantly boost your savings over time. Tax-free is fantastic.

2. Research reputable investment companies such as T. Rowe Price, Fidelity, and Charles Schwab, among others. These companies are recognized for their competitive fees, diverse investment options, and exceptional customer service. I don't have an endorsement

from any company, but these are good places to start your research.

3. Look into a four- or five-star mutual fund that you see in the company you are researching and double-check it with Morningstar and other mutual fund evaluators. If you're not familiar with these terms or this concept, you can look them up online. There are resources to help you. Be sure to examine one-year, three-year, five-year, and lifetime returns. Considering a mutual fund's performance over just the last three months or one year can be misleading. It's essential to examine the fund's performance over a more extended period to obtain a more accurate picture of its potential returns.

4. When you find a good index mutual fund, you will set up an account with the company and deposit your money into the fund you have chosen. Contact a

company, and they will be happy to assist you.

5. You need to set up automatic withdrawals from a savings or checking account for $100 per month, which will be deposited directly into your account each month for the next 30 years. Your mindset should be that this is a bill, and I owe it to myself and my future. I will never use or withdraw this money until I am 59 and a half years old.

6. You may have to make some small sacrifices along the way that seem essential, but they won't seem so important when you start to see the money compound and add up in your Roth IRA account. Just work more if you want more fun money. You get one chance at this, and when you're young, time is your ally in helping you save. The longer you wait to start investing, the more costly it will become in many ways.

7. Lastly, do not plan to touch this money; not for a new car, house, boat, or anything. Think of it as money you never had. It may require some sacrifices, but it will be worth it. Do the math for yourself—the results are powerful.

What lies behind us and what lies before us are tiny matters compared to what lies within us.

—Ralph Waldo Emerson

Your One-Degree Shift

- Talk to a trusted adult about the concept of a Roth IRA.

- When you get paid or receive money, immediately put 10 percent of it into a savings account before you spend anything else.

Conclusion

In Closing: Your Journey Begins Now

As we draw this book to a close, let's look back at where we've been. We began by understanding that average is crowded, and you were meant for more. From my own struggles with a 1.67 GPA to the life-changing power of a single mentor, you've seen that your starting point does not determine your destination.

The core message of this book is that you are in control. The foundation you build with anchor habits—sleep, nutrition, reading—is your launchpad. The mindset you cultivate, centered on greatness, honor, and discipline, serves as your guiding system. The toolkit you've gathered provides you with practical strategies to turn your goals into reality.

You now understand that motivation is a spark, but discipline is the engine. You know that belonging is better than fitting in. Most importantly, you know that the person you become tomorrow is determined by the deposits you make today. You're the author of your story, the one in the arena, the person in charge.

This is not the end. It's the starting line. The trek to defy average is a daily commitment to becoming the person you're meant to be.

An Afterword:
Notes from Two Students

Throughout the process of writing this book, I had the privilege of working with two exceptional high school students, Maryum Ahmed and Sophia Memon. They served as my alpha readers, which means they were the first to read the manuscript, offer critical feedback, and help shape the final version you hold in your hands.

Their insights were invaluable, but I soon realized that their authentic perspective as students navigating the challenges of high school *at the moment* was too powerful not to share directly with you. They graciously agreed to write this section from their perspective.

These are their words, their experiences, and their advice to you, their peers. I hope you find their wisdom as inspiring as I have.

— Scott Zellmann

A Letter from Two High School Students

By Maryum Ahmed and Sophia Memon (email message to author, September 12, 2025)

We've been helping edit this book and were asked to share some of our authentic experiences.

Consistency

The key to success in anything, especially high school, is consistency. Being consistent means choosing something you're passionate about and sticking with it, even when you're tired, motivated, sad, overwhelmed, or disinterested in the moment. Choosing discipline over motivation will produce long-term results. An example of this could be a club. You attend the first meeting and think it's great, but then you start to lose motivation, so you skip the next meeting. One thing leads to another, and you stop going entirely. Or say your friend doesn't go, you think you can't go without them. So you stop showing up. This loss of discipline is why you can't achieve what you want. Things are easier said than done. If you want to improve at anything, you have to put consistency, effort, and discipline into it. When you decide not to show up, not give your best, or to slack off, there will always be someone else who puts in 100 percent. If you stray from your plan, don't beat yourself up, but hold yourself accountable. Recognize that the choice you made probably wasn't the best one, but then forgive yourself and promise to do better. When you make a promise to yourself, keep it. Showing up to the gym when you're not at 100 percent and having a mediocre workout is always better than skipping entirely and lying on your couch. Similarly, attending class when you feel drained will benefit you more than skipping and getting in trouble.

Just because your energy levels aren't high and you don't feel your best doesn't mean that the world stops turning. It's okay to acknowledge "Today isn't my best day," and then decide to still go about it as usual. One thing I like to remember is to keep my long-term goals in mind. Say an episode of your favorite show dropped, but you have to go to the gym to train for your sport after school. While your heart may want to stay home to watch the episode, your discipline should drive you to the gym. In a few months, watching the show a day late isn't going to have an effect. If you had gone to the gym instead that day, you could've hit a PR in your training.

Self-Doubt

A significant challenge I face daily is overcoming self-doubt and learning to push past it. I still constantly overthink and tell myself little things like "I can't do this" or "I give up." Those small moments of self-doubt lead to a pit of thinking that you're incapable of achieving success. Shift your perspective to thinking, "I will try my best," or simply saying to yourself, "I can do this," before taking a test, working out, or even while doing homework. You must have confidence and trust yourself to believe you **can** do it. A familiar feeling among high schoolers is imposter syndrome, a psychological phenomenon in which people doubt their own skills and successes, feeling like frauds. This is an extreme form of self-doubt, but it is a common phenomenon. Just know that you aren't the only one who experiences this, and the skills you have or classes you're in, you're deserving of being in. The work you've put in in previous years has led you to the right place; you are where you're meant to be. Don't tell yourself, "The other kids on varsity are better." You are on varsity. You're there because the coach decided you have what it takes. Don't undermine the work you've put in by comparing yourself with others.

Comparison

Theodore Roosevelt said, "Comparison is the thief of joy." I think in high school, especially, it becomes challenging not to compare yourself to others. Others have nicer clothes, better style, are smarter, more athletic, have more friends, but it doesn't matter. How do you know you are not the object of someone else's envy? You don't know that other kids at school don't walk past you and compare themselves to you. The point is, I think happiness is unattainable until you decide to focus on you and only you. What others do doesn't determine what you need to do, and no two paths look the same for each person. Instead of wasting your time cutting yourself down because someone else gets more playing time or attention from a coach or teacher, figure out what they're doing that you're not. You can truly shine when you're not being held back by the fear of what others are doing.

Don't be afraid to do what you know you need. An example I often see is in the weight room. The coaches will give us a four-block workout circuit, with each block featuring different exercises. As the clock nears 5:30 p.m., most of the team is checked out and getting ready to leave. They'll usually skip the last circuit or not complete it. If you know that the previous exercises in the circuit are going to be beneficial to you, it doesn't matter if everyone else has decided they're done. You're not *weird* for actually completing the workout, and if others think you're a "try hard," then they're not trying hard enough.

Friendship

When you're in high school, your motivation levels can get low. You're busy with school, sports, social pressure, and trying to balance your own values while also fitting in. No one wants to feel "weird." Everyone craves the feeling of inclusion and belonging, and sometimes you're forced to compromise what you really believe in to continue to succeed within a social circle. One of the most significant things I've learned in high school is that the people you surround yourself with are important. If the people around you or the situations you find yourself in are leading you to compromise your values, you need to remove yourself from those surroundings. Being around people who are into things that are negatively impacting them, at one point or another, is going to become who you are. Your close friends should be people you can trust. Your best friend shouldn't be someone who you are worried about spilling your secrets or corrupting you with bad choices. Similarly, if you haven't yet found people you genuinely connect with, don't rush it. Don't push yourself to make "good friends" who don't really care about you. A small, genuine circle will always be better than a large group of people who pretend to like each other.

Values

A person's most important quality is their values. People will compromise kindness, and they'll compromise their discipline, but when I see someone doing something they know in their heart is wrong, it makes me wary of them. Because of this, I believe friends are incredibly important because they are an extension of oneself. If your close friends are all unmotivated, lazy people, that is precisely what you're going to become. Their values will align with yours. At the end of the day, when you're old and high school doesn't matter anymore, when people remember you, what do you want them to think of? A mean, cold, inconsiderate person? Or a warm, welcoming, kind person? Your values determine these things. My mom has always told me, "People will forget what you did, what you said; but people will never forget how you made them feel." Be someone who makes others feel good, not someone who brings people down.

Coping

One of my most significant pieces of advice for all high school students is to find a coping mechanism. When you're in a bad mood or a bad place, and you need to reset your mindset, what do you do? Some people stress-eat, some people cry, and some people shop; for me, I prefer to exercise. The first thing I do when I feel like my brain is jumbled and I'm stressed and upset is to move my body. I enjoy walking, running, and going to the gym, and I almost always end my workouts with a clearer mind. Find something that calms you down and quiets your mind. I utilize various forms of exercise to enhance other aspects of my life. When I'm stressed out and need to shut my brain off, I'll lift weights. I have to put in effort to maintain my form correctly and lift heavy weights, and my brain focuses entirely on that. On the other hand, if I need to process something and really dissect a situation or problem, I like to walk. I'll put my headphones in and walk around my neighborhood, which gives me time to sort out what I need to do in a healthy way.

Procrastination

Don't do it. I know that's a lot easier said than done, but if you tell yourself, "I'm not going to procrastinate today when I get home from school, and I'm going to finish my homework so I can go to sleep early tonight," then follow through on it. Take the steps to follow through on what you said you would do. Leave your phone in another room, go to a place without distractions, and focus. This being said, be realistic. If you have three hours of homework, you won't go home straight from school and do it all in one sitting. Plan breaks and set timers. Setting timers is one of the easiest ways for me to stay within a time limit. And, if you set a timer, respect it. If the timer rings and you continue to take your break, then what was the point of setting it in the first place? As someone who used to write essays the morning of and complete projects the night before due dates, I understand how easy it's to get sucked into doing things at the last minute. In the end, it doesn't really come down to the grade you get on the project. If you had three weeks to write an essay and completed it in three hours before it was due, still managing to get an A, that's great, but it's not something to be proud of. You're essentially celebrating the fact that you put in less than your best and still managed to pull a good grade. If you had worked on the assignment a little each day since it was assigned and completed it a week early, that would be something to be proud of. You effectively managed your time, and your hard work paid off.

One thing that has really helped me is doing my homework the day it's assigned.

Whether it's due the next day, in two days, or a week, if it's something I can do in one night, I'll do it the day I get it. Then, I'm stress-free until the due date. Practicing good time management skills will benefit you for the rest of your life. If I continued my habit of procrastination, I would have carried it with me throughout college and any subsequent schooling.

Additionally, my poor time management skills began to seep into other areas of my life. I would always be late for school, hangouts with friends, and any party or event I attended. That is still an issue for me. I continue to struggle with time management, but I actively work toward bettering myself each day, and I've seen results. The takeaway? Kill bad habits now. Don't be the person who doesn't realize how negatively what they've been doing has impacted them until it's too late.

References

For those who wish to delve deeper into the ideas discussed in this book, these sources and recommended readings inspired me to write this book, and I hope they inspire you as well.

- Clear, James. *Atomic Habits*. Avery, 2018.
- Covey, Stephen R. *The 7 Habits of Highly Effective People*. Simon & Schuster, 2020.
- Duckworth, Angela. *Grit: The Power of Passion and Perseverance*. Scribner, 2016.
- Duhigg, Charles. *The Power of Habit*. Random House, 2012.
- Frankl, Viktor E. *Man's Search for Meaning*. Beacon Press, 2006.

- Goggins, David. *Never Finished.* Lioncrest Publishing, 2022.
- Helmstetter, Shad. *What to Say When You Talk to Your Self.* Thorsons, 2017.
- Ledbetter, Brett. *What Drives Winning.* Green Dot Publishing, 2016.
- Willink, Jocko. *Extreme Ownership.* St. Martin's Press, 2015.

Acknowledgments

This book would not have been possible without the encouragement and support of many people.

To my loving family: **Sheron, Sarah, Sydney, and my son-in-law, Ethan**—thank you for asking questions, listening to my vision, and giving me the quiet time I needed to follow this dream. To Sarah and Ethan, I am so excited to welcome **Beckham** into our family.

Thank you to my mom and dad, Linda, my brothers, Bobby and Mike, and my sister, Andrea. You all have been a blessing.

I would like to extend special thanks to my alpha readers, **Maryum Ahmed and Sophia Memon**. Without your constant dedication and hard work, this book would not have turned out as well as it did. I am incredibly proud of all you contributed. You are both outstanding trailblazers, and I was blessed to witness your fantastic work. I am forever indebted to you.

I would like to extend a special thank you to an **anonymous alpha reader** whose early feedback was crucial in shaping this book.

Finally, to all my beta readers, thank you. Your thoughtful feedback was invaluable in sharpening the final manuscript and catching the details I missed. I am so grateful for your time and insight, especially to **Karen Zellmann, Mark Richter, Allison Gustilo, Carol Etherton, and Inayah Mohammed. Maggie** strong!

www.ingramcontent.com/pod-product-compliance
Lightning Source LLC
Chambersburg PA
CBHW020427130626
46549CB00001B/14